NUMBER POWER

A Cooperative Approach to Mathematics and Social Development

Laurel Robertson
Shaila Regan
Marji Freeman
Susan Urquhart-Brown

Addison-Wesley Publishing Company
Menlo Park, California ■ Reading, Massachusetts ■ New York
Don Mills, Ontario ■ Wokingham, England ■ Amsterdam
Bonn ■ Sydney ■ Singapore ■ Tokyo ■ Madrid ■ San Juan
Paris ■ Seoul, Korea ■ Milan ■ Mexico City ■ Taipei, Taiwan

Funded through a grant by the Stuart Foundations of San Francisco, *Number Power* was developed by the The Cooperative Mathematics Project, a program of the Developmental Studies Center, 111 Deerwood Place, Suite 165, San Ramon, California 94583.

Managing Editor: Michael Kane
Project Editor: Mali Apple
Production: Barbara Atmore
Design: Don Taka
Illustrations: Duane Bibby
Cover Art: Terry Guyer

The blackline masters in this publication are designed to be used with appropriate duplicating equipment to produce copies for classroom use. Addison-Wesley Publishing Company grants permission to classroom teachers to reproduce these masters.

Copyright © 1993 by Addison-Wesley Publishing Company, Inc.
Printed in the United States of America.

ISBN 0-201-45523-4

1 2 3 4 5 6 7 8 9 10-ML-96 95 94 93 92

Contents

Acknowledgments — iv
About the Authors — vi
Preface — vii
Number Sense and Social Development — viii
Using Cooperative Group Work
 in Your Classroom — x
Number Power Format — xv

Unit 1
Fraction Explorations

Overview — 1
Lesson 1: Team Emblem — 7
Lesson 2: Lemonade — 13
Lesson 3: Nutty Cookies! — 17
Lesson 4: Sharing Candy Bars — 23
Lesson 5: Paper Strips — 29
Lesson 6: Cars and Ramps — 35
Lesson 7: Geoboards 1 — 41
Lesson 8: Geoboards 2 — 47
Lesson 9: Geoboards 3 — 55
Lesson 10: Plant a Garden — 63

Unit 2
Fractions: Parts and Wholes

Overview — 69
Lesson 1: Fraction Puzzles — 75
Lesson 2: Advertisements — 81
Lesson 3: Fraction Kits — 85
Lesson 4: Fractions, Fractions! — 91
Lesson 5: Spin It — 97
Lesson 6: Say It with Fractions — 105
Lesson 7: Pencil Investigations 1 — 111
Lesson 8: Pencil Investigations 2 — 117
Lesson 9: Pencil Investigations 3 — 121
Lesson 10: What Do You Think? — 125

Unit 3
Large Numbers

Overview — 131
Lesson 1: Find Someone Who…! — 137
Lesson 2: What Makes Sense? — 143
Lesson 3: A Million Bucks 1 — 147
Lesson 4: Facts About Numbers — 157
Lesson 5: Wipe Out — 161
Lesson 6: Guesswork — 171
Lesson 7: A Million Bucks 2 — 177
Lesson 8: Large-Number Buddies — 181

Additional Reading — 185

Acknowledgments

Many people were involved in the development and production of *Number Power*. We are grateful for their time, valuable suggestions, and encouragement.

In particular, we wish to express our deep appreciation to the Stuart Foundations of San Francisco and to Ted Lobman, president, for their faith in and support of our program.

We extend our sincere thanks to the Walter S. Johnson Foundation and staff, who provided not only encouragement, but also a bridging grant at a critical time.

We also wish to thank the members of our Advisory Board, who contributed enormously to the development of the *Number Power* program:

Joan Akers, California State Department of Education

Carne Barnett, Far West Laboratory for Educational Research and Development

Neil Davidson, University of Maryland

Carol Langbort, San Francisco State University

Nell Noddings, Stanford University

Ruth Parker, Collaborative Learning Associates, Ferndale, Washington

Paul Trafton, University of Northern Iowa

Jean Stenmark, EQUALS, Lawrence Hall of Science, University of California, Berkeley

Many teachers piloted lessons and units, allowed us in their classrooms to teach or to observe, and provided us with feedback that helped shape the format and content of the program. We particularly wish to acknowledge the following teachers and math specialists:

California

Alameda City Unified School District
Jane Baldi

Albany City Unified School District
Nancy Johnson
Violet Nicholas
Susie Ronfeldt

Berkeley Unified School District
Carolyn Adams
Mary Ough

Moreland Elementary School District
Terry Baker
Pat Brigham
Wanda Binford
Cristine Bryant
Carolyn Cassell
Shari Clare
Jan Frosberg
Vivian Karpel
Lew Osborn
Terry Pomposo
Linda Stumpf
Gaby Tennant

Oakland Unified School District
Mike Butzen
Roz Haberkern
Alicia Rivera
Kathy Selleck
Ted Sugarman
Sue Tierney

Redwood City Elementary School District
Kris Dalrymple
Lisa Erskine
Frances Nuss
Ann Marie Sulzbach

Ross Elementary School District
Allison Quoyeser

John Swett Unified School District
Kay Balandra
Louise Bevilaqua
Julie Contestable
Alice Dorman
Marilyn Griego
Anita Pister
Jackie Schlemmer
Carol Westrich

San Ramon Valley Unified School District
Cindy Collins
Cheryl Gonzales
Deneka Horaleck
Lincoln Olbrycht
Sally Powers
Sue Smith
Ruby Tellsworth

Stockton City Unified School District
Jan Holloway

Vallejo City Unified School District
Howard Banford

Canada

School District No. 39, Vancouver, British Columbia
Shirley Brunke
Pat Craig
Joan Crockett
Wayne Gatley
Liz Gautschi
Linda O'Reilly
Jan Renouf
Carrie Sleep

We would also like to thank the authors of the following resources from which we adapted a number of lessons:

A Collection of Math Lessons Grades 3 to 6 by Marilyn Burns (Sausalito, CA: The Math Solution Publications, 1987)

The Math Solution: Teaching Mathematics Through Problem Solving by Marilyn Burns (Sausalito, CA: Marilyn Burns Education Associates, 1984)

EQUALS: Use EQUALS to Promote the Participation of Women in Mathematics by Alice Kaseberg, Nancy Kreinberg, and Diane Downie (Berkeley, CA: Regents of the University of California, 1980)

Used Numbers: Real Data in the Classroom by Susan Jo Russell, Rebecca Corwin, and Susan Friel. (Palo Alto, CA: Dale Seymour Publications, 1990)

Teaching Kids Math by Carne Barnett (Englewood Cliffs, NJ: Prentice Hall, Inc., 1982)

The staff at Addison-Wesley was an additional source of guidance for us. In particular, we wish to thank the following:

Stuart Brewster, Publisher
Michael Kane, Managing Editor
Mali Apple, Editor
Barbara Atmore, Production Coordinator

Finally, we wish to thank the staff of the Developmental Studies Center, particularly the following people, for their support and invaluable contributions:

Eric Schaps, President
Anne Goddard, Publications Editor
Lynn Murphy, Publications Editor
Susan Frost, Production Editor
Caroline Arakelian, Copy Editor
Peter Cole, Copy Editor
Julie Contestable, Curriculum Developer
Bill Ruano, Curriculum Developer
Allan Ferguson, Computer Specialist
Patrick Kammermeyer, Computer Specialist
Joanne Slaboch, Administrator
Dan Solomon, Director of Research
Carol Stone, Evaluator
Margaret Tauber, Evaluator
Betsy Franco, Writing Consultant
Duane Bibby, Illustrator
Stella McCloskey, Administrative Assistant
Denise Wood, Administrative Assistant

About the Authors

Laurel Robertson
Director

Dr. Robertson has been in education for more than twenty years as a classroom teacher, staff developer, mathematics consultant, and director of several educational programs. She is past president of the California Association for Cooperation in Education and is currently on the board of directors of the International Association for the Study of Cooperation in Education.

Shaila Regan
Curriculum Developer

Ms. Regan has extensive experience as an elementary school mathematics specialist and classroom teacher. She has also been a mathematics consultant and staff developer for public and private schools throughout the United States, and is past president of the Alameda/Contra Costa Counties Mathematics Educators.

Marji Freeman
Curriculum Developer

Ms. Freeman has more than fifteen years' experience as a middle-school mathematics teacher and mathematics consultant. In 1986, she received the Texas State Presidential Award in Mathematics Teaching. Ms. Freeman is an instructor for Marilyn Burns Education Associates, consultant to Cuisenaire Company of America, and author of *Creative Graphing* (Cuisenaire Company of America, 1986).

Susan Urquhart-Brown
Curriculum Developer

Ms. Urquhart-Brown has been in education for more than twenty years. In addition to having taught in preschool, elementary, and secondary schools, she has designed and conducted a parent education program, and directed a mathematics professional development program for teachers.

Preface

This is an exciting time to be a mathematics teacher. Educators and the general public alike are calling for fundamental changes in the content and process of mathematics instruction. Recent national reports document the need for change, describe new goals for the field, and suggest new approaches to teaching and learning.

Number Power is designed to meet the call for curricula that models new instructional strategies and content. The focus of the program is to support and expand students' emerging number sense. The *Number Power* program consists of three multiweek units each for kindergarten through grade six and is intended to supplement or replace existing curricula aimed at developing number concepts.

The *Number Power* units provide opportunities for all students to construct and expand their understanding of number over time, as they engage in and reflect on experiences that help them make mathematical connections, employ mathematical tools, work with others to solve problems, and communicate about their thinking. The units are designed to be accessible to all students and to meet the needs of students with diverse backgrounds and experiences. Each unit fosters the development of several essential concepts and may include other areas of mathematics, such as measurement, geometry, and data analysis.

Number Power takes a holistic, developmental view of education and is designed to enhance students' social, as well as mathematical, development. Cooperative group work and ongoing discussion about group interaction help students understand the need to be fair, caring, and responsible, and develop the skills needed to work successfully with others.

Number Sense and Social Development

Number Power is based on the assumption that we learn about the world through everyday interaction with our environment and with others. Academic and social learning are integrated naturally, rather than developed in isolation from each other. Exploration, questioning, discussion, and reasoning are all part of this natural learning process that begins at birth.

With this assumption in mind, *Number Power* has been designed to support students' mathematical and social development in an integrated manner by actively engaging them in exploration and reasoning with others. Students in pairs and in groups investigate open-ended questions; use a wide variety of tools; develop problem-solving strategies; collect, organize, and analyze data; and record and communicate their thinking and results. Students' sense of number is fostered along with their understanding of what it means to be fair, caring, and responsible and their disposition and ability to act on these values.

Number Sense

A sound understanding of number is indispensible to making sense of the world. Documents such as *Curriculum and Evaluation Standards for School Mathematics* (National Council of Teachers of Mathematics, 1989) and *Reshaping School Mathematics* (Mathematical Sciences Education Board, 1990) make it clear that the development of students' number sense should be a primary goal of elementary school mathematics programs.

The focus of *Number Power* is to develop students' number sense. In particular, the program is designed to enhance students' understanding of number meaning and relationships, the relative magnitude of number, the effects and relative relationships of operations, and referents for quantities and measures. *Number Power* is also designed to enhance students' abilities to apply these concepts to everyday problems.

Students come to school with some understanding of the meaning of numbers, of how numbers relate to each other, and of how numbers can be used to describe quantities. *Number Power* extends this conceptual understanding by providing opportunities for students to explore and use numbers as they solve problems, discuss their thinking, and make connections between their experience and the underlying concepts.

This cycle of concrete experiences and reflection on these experiences also enhances students' sense of the relative magnitude of whole numbers, decimals, and fractions. Students begin to understand, for example, that 24 is two twelves, almost 25, about half of 50, small compared with 93, and large compared with 3. They also begin to develop "benchmarks"—recognizing, for example, that 0.8 is closer to 1.0 than to 0.5.

Number Power strives to deepen students' understanding of how operations affect numbers— how, for example, adding 4 to 24 results in a far smaller change in the number than does multiplying 24 by 4. Students have opportunities to develop their own algorithms and to begin to develop a sense of the effect of using a number as an operator on other numbers—understanding, for example, what happens when a number is multiplied by 0 or divided by 1.

Number Power involves students in experiences that help them relate numbers to the real world. As a result of experiences such as these, students begin to develop appropriate referents for numbers used in everyday life and to develop a range of possible quantities and measures for everyday situations. They begin to recognize, for example, that a dog would not weigh 800 pounds or that it is reasonable that a new car would cost about $15,000.

Number Power provides opportunities for students to apply their understanding of number to problems and to everyday situations. Students collect, organize, and interpret data, and develop their own informal ways to compute. Within a variety of problem-solving and real-life contexts—such as cooking, surveying class members about their pets, or making a quilt—students are encouraged to

- make estimates;
- decide when an estimate or an exact answer is appropriate;
- make sense of numbers and judge the reasonableness of solutions;
- use numbers to support an argument; and
- make decisions about the appropriate use of different computational methods—calculator, pencil and paper, or mental computation.

Social Development

Traditionally, schools have taken a major role in the socialization of students, helping them become responsible citizens. In recent decades, this role has taken a backseat to academic preparation, as students and schools have been judged almost entirely by their success in meeting narrow academic standards.

Today, however, the stresses of our rapidly changing world require schools to refocus attention on students' social development while continuing to support their academic development. In order to prepare students for the challenges of the next century, schools must help them

- be creative, thoughtful, and knowledgeable;
- develop a lifelong love of learning and the ability to pursue their own learning goals;
- be principled, responsible, and humane; and
- be able to work effectively with others to solve problems.

The recognition that social development and academic learning are integral to schooling and occur simultaneously is a cornerstone of *Number Power*.

In each lesson, students have opportunities to explore and solve problems with others and to discuss and reflect on their group interaction. In the process, students are encouraged to balance their own needs with the needs of others, to recognize how their behavior affects others, to think about the underlying values that guide behavior, and to develop appropriate group skills. Reflection on their experience helps students construct their understanding of social and cultural norms, and leads to a deeper integration of positive social values in their lives.

Using Cooperative Group Work in Your Classroom

Cooperative group work benefits all students, both academically and socially. When students with different abilities, backgrounds, and perspectives explain their thinking and listen to the thinking of others, their reasoning and communication skills are fostered. Additionally, they are exposed to new ideas and strategies, learn to be supportive of and to value others, and become more positive about themselves as learners and more motivated to learn.

What Is the *Number Power* Approach?

The *Number Power* approach to cooperative group work includes some elements common to most cooperative learning methods: students work in heterogeneous pairs or groups as they pursue a common goal, are actively involved in their learning, and have ongoing opportunities to share ideas, discuss their thinking, and hear the thinking of others.

The *Number Power* approach differs from other cooperative learning methods in several respects, but especially in its focus on social development. Beyond addressing group skills, *Number Power* places particular emphasis on encouraging students to be responsible for their own learning and behavior, and on helping students construct their understanding of

- what it means to be fair, caring, and responsible;
- why these values are important; and
- how these values can be acted on in their daily lives.

Another difference is that the *Number Power* approach does not specify role assignments for group work. Instead, the lessons provide opportunities for students to decide such things as how they will divide the work or how they will record and report their findings. Learning how to make these decisions helps students become responsible group members. Many of the lessons include examples of questions that help students think about how they made these decisions and what they learned that would help them the next time they work together.

The *Number Power* approach does not recommend that student work be graded. The goal of the lessons is to support conceptual development. The lessons are designed to be learning experiences rather than experiences that expect student mastery and strive to encourage exploration, creativity, and intrinsic motivation. Concern about grades can greatly inhibit students' willingness to take risks and explore alternative strategies. *Number Power* lessons do, however, provide many opportunities for ongoing assessment of student understanding.

Throughout all aspects of the *Number Power* lessons, the asking of probing, open-ended questions is paramount to helping students construct their understanding. The questions suggested in the lessons seldom have a single right answer. Many are focused on helping students examine and rely on the authority of their own thinking. If students are used to answering recall questions or to giving an answer that they think the teacher wants, they may initially fail to understand the questions or meet them with silence or irrelevant answers. Their willingness to risk will increase as they understand that explaining their thinking and sharing many strategies and solutions is valued and important. Their ability to explain their thinking will increase with practice.

Many of the *Number Power* lessons suggest the use of some easily implemented cooperative learning strategies that provide opportunities for students to share their thinking. (For more information about cooperative strategies, Kagan's *Cooperative*

Learning is particularly informative. See Additional Reading, p. 185.)

1. ***Turn to Your Partner.*** Students turn to a person sitting next to them to discuss an issue or question.

2. ***Heads Together.*** Students in groups of four put their heads together to discuss an issue or question among themselves.

3. ***Think, Pair, Share.*** Students individually take a short period of time to think about a question or issue and then discuss their thoughts with a partner. The pair reports its thinking to another pair or to the class.

4. ***Think, Pair, Write.*** This structure is like "Think, Pair, Share," except the pairs write about their thinking after they have discussed their thoughts. This writing then might be shared with you, with another pair, or with the class.

5. ***Group Brainstorming.*** In this structure, each group needs someone to record ideas. Groups are given some time to come up with as many ideas as they can about a topic or a problem, and the recorder lists all ideas. Then groups are given time to analyze, synthesize, and prioritize their ideas.

The *Number Power* approach recognizes that a strong mathematics program will include a variety of instructional methods. The program, therefore, includes some direct instruction and individual work in addition to cooperative group work.

How Are *Number Power* Lessons Structured?

Number Power lessons are structured to provide frequent opportunities for students to interact with each other and with the teacher. Group work and class discussion alternate throughout the lessons. Many lessons begin with a class discussion about such things as the goals of the lesson and how they fit with previous work, the mathematical and social emphases of the lesson, and the problem or activity. During group work, students are asked open-ended questions to extend their thinking, to help them solve problems, or to informally assess their concept development. At times, the class meets to discuss strategies and solutions, and often new questions. The lesson concludes with an opportunity for groups and the class to reflect on their mathematical work and social interaction.

How Do I Begin?

Whether or not you have used cooperative learning strategies before, it is a good idea to start slowly. Begin with pairs rather than larger group sizes. Try some of the strategies suggested in the previous section. These and other strategies can be used as part of the teaching and learning experience in any subject and can be used to structure student interaction before, during, and after traditional or cooperative lessons.

An important factor in helping students become responsible, independent, and cooperative learners is the establishment of an environment that supports cooperation. A supportive environment makes students feel safe, values and respects their efforts and opinions, and provides them with many opportunities to make choices and decisions. The role you play and what you model are crucial to the development of this environment. For example, asking questions that help students solve a problem on their own encourages them to become responsible for their learning and shows that you value their ability to do so. Asking open-ended questions beginning with such words as what, why, or how helps students extend their understanding and become confident in their abilities. Likewise, asking for a variety of solutions to a problem and for explanations of how they were derived helps students understand that risk-taking is desirable, that you are not just looking for a "right" answer, and that you value their thinking. Also, encouraging students to respectfully ask each other questions about their strategies creates a safe environment for constructive disagreement.

The physical setup of the room is also an important factor. The arrangement should allow group members to have access to materials and to be able to communicate with each other easily. Sharing one desk or small table, or sitting at two desks side-by-side, is a good arrangement for a pair; a small table or a cluster of desks works well for a group of four.

Learning to cooperate is a developmental process and can be difficult for students, especially in the beginning. Students may, for example, have trouble balancing their own needs with those of others, taking responsibility for their work and behavior, or dealing with open-ended questions. Understanding that these difficulties are a valuable part of the learning process will help both you and your students be more comfortable.

Class Building

At the beginning of the year in particular, it is important to help students develop a sense of identity and community as a group in order to support and develop a sense of cooperation. Students need ongoing opportunities to learn about each other, to set norms for behavior, and to make decisions about their classroom. Activities such as developing a class name, logo, or handshake can lead to an "our classroom" feeling. (Many ideas for class-building activities can be found in such resources as Graves' *A Part to Play*, Mormon and Dishon's *Our Classroom*, Rhodes and McCabe's *The Nurturing Classroom*, and Gibbs and Allen's *Tribes*. See Additional Reading, p. 185.)

Class building is an ongoing process; the spirit of community needs to be developed and supported throughout the year. Class-building activities are particularly important after a long vacation, after you have been absent for an extended period of time, after illness has kept many students home, or when you have an influx of new students.

Forming Groups

Several decisions need to be made regarding group formation: the size of the groups, how to form them, and how long to keep them together. The *Number Power* program suggests a group size for each lesson, and that students be randomly assigned to groups that work together for an entire unit.

A major benefit of randomly assigning students to groups is that it gives several positive messages to students: there is no hidden agenda behind how you grouped students (such as choosing groups based on student achievement); every student is considered a valuable group member; and everyone is expected to learn to work with everyone else. Randomly assigning students also results in heterogenous groups, important for cooperative group work, even though at times a group may be homogenous in some way; for example, all girls or all boys. The following are several ways to randomly group students. (Other suggestions can be found in the Johnsons' *Circle of Learning*. See Additional Reading, p. 185.)

1. Have students number off and have the ones form a group, the twos form a group, and so on.

2. Have students take a playing card or an ice cream stick with a number on it and find others with the same number.

3. Have students take a card with an equation or short word problem on it and form a group with others who have an equation or word problem with the same solution.

4. Cut magazine pictures into the same number of pieces as members in a group. Have students pick a piece and find others with pieces of the same puzzle.

Keeping groups together for an entire unit provides an opportunity for students to develop and expand their interpersonal skills and their understanding of group interaction. Students learn to work through and learn from problems, and to build on successful methods of interaction. Long-term group work also allows students to build on their mathematical discoveries.

Team Building

Each time new long-term groups are formed, it is important to provide opportunities for students to get better acquainted, to develop a sense of identity as a team, and to begin to develop their working relationship. Each *Number Power* unit begins with a team-building activity. (The references suggested under Class Building also are good sources for additional team-building activities.)

During team-building activities, helping students label, discuss, and analyze behavior lays a foundation for their future group work. Open-ended questions can draw students' attention to their interaction, to their behavior that helps the group, and to how they might solve problems that have arisen.

Such questions might, for example, encourage students to talk about how they worked together; what group skills they used; how they wish to treat each other; why it is important to be fair, caring, and responsible; what problems they had; and the ways they wish to work together the next time.

What Is My Role?

One of the main goals of cooperative group work is to encourage students to do their own thinking and to take responsibility for their own learning. Your role is vital to the process of students becoming independent and interdependent learners. In addition to setting the environment for cooperation, this role includes planning and introducing the lesson, facilitating group work, helping students reflect, and helping students say good-bye.

Planning

Reading a *Number Power* unit, Overview and lessons, prior to implementation will help you make decisions about how to connect the lessons with students' previous experiences, and about the social values and group skills that might be emphasized throughout the unit. The group skills listed on the first page of each lesson are suggestions based on the type of student interaction that might occur in that lesson. (Listening skills, for example, might be the focus of a lesson in which students are explaining their thinking to others.) However, the developmental level of your students, their previous cooperative group experiences, and level of cooperation they demonstrate may lead you to choose other skills as a focus. You might also wish to develop a theme for a unit, such as communicating with others.

The following list of questions may help you as you plan. The *Number Power* lessons incorporate suggestions for many of them.

- What are the important *mathematical concepts* of the lesson? How are they linked with previous work and long-term goals?
- What are some possible opportunities for supporting social, as well as mathematical, learning?
- Is the lesson *interesting, accessible,* and *challenging* for all students? What modifications are needed?
- What *room arrangement* will be best for the lesson?
- What *materials* will be needed for the lesson?
- How will time for *student discussion* and *work* be maximized?
- How will *interdependence* among group members be encouraged?
- How will the lesson provide opportunities for students to *make decisions* and *take responsibility* for their learning and behavior?
- What will you be looking for as you *observe* group work?
- What *open-ended questions* might extend students' thinking?
- How will *assessment* be linked with instruction?
- What are appropriate *extension activities* for groups that finish early or for the next day?

Introducing the Lesson

Many *Number Power* lessons begin with questions that ask students to reflect on previous lessons or experiences, or pose a problem for students to discuss. Such questions are often followed with discussion about a problem or investigation that students will undertake and about specific cooperative group skills that might help them work effectively.

Discussing group skills at the beginning of the lesson provides students with models for positive interaction and with language to discuss their interaction. Vary the way these group skills are discussed. You might choose, for example, to emphasize a skill such as listening to others, then have students discuss what it means to listen, how others will know that they are being listened to, how listening might help their group work, and how listening to others relates to the values of being fair, caring, and responsible. You might, instead, ask groups to discuss and choose skills that they think are important to the functioning of their group, or ask students to discuss what they have learned about working together that will help them in this new lesson. At other times, you could have students role-play the activity and then, as a class, discuss what they observed about the group interaction and what group skills they think might be particularly important to their work. For some lessons, you might choose not to discuss group interaction at all during the introduction. No matter how and when you choose to discuss the social emphases of the lesson and the group skills with students, it is important to remember that social understanding is constructed through many opportunities to work with others and reflect on their experience.

Facilitating Group Work

During group work, ask thoughtful, probing, open-ended questions. The focus of such questions is to help students define the problems they are investigating, to help them solve interpersonal problems, to help them take responsibility for their learning and behavior, and to extend and informally assess their thinking.

As students begin group work, observe each group to be sure that students have understood the task and have no insurmountable problems; then focus on a few groups and observe each of them long enough to see what is really happening. This will provide you with information about students' ability to work together, their involvement in the activity, and their mathematical and social understanding. Such observation will also give you ideas for questions you might ask, and help you determine what other experiences students may need.

At times during group work, you may decide to intervene to refocus a group, to help them see a problem from another perspective, to ask questions that extend mathematical and social learning, or to assess understanding. When you intervene to assess or extend thinking, try not to interrupt the flow of the group work. Wait for a natural pause in the action. Ask open-ended questions that require progressively more thought or understanding. (Each *Number Power* lesson suggests sample questions to probe students' thinking about number and number relationships, to help them think about how they are solving problems, and to help them analyze their group work.) If a group is having difficulty, allow members time to solve a problem themselves before you intervene. Then, ask key questions to help them resolve the difficulty, rather than solving the problem for them or giving lengthy explanations.

Helping Students Reflect

Reflection on the mathematical and social aspects of group work helps students develop their conceptual understanding, build on past learning experiences, and connect their experience to long-term learning goals. Questioning before, during, and after group work encourages students to consider such important issues as, "What does it mean to be responsible?" and "How did my behavior affect others in the group?" and extends their mathematical thinking. *Number Power* lessons incorporate several methods to structure ongoing reflection, including group discussion, writing, and whole-class discussions. Each *Number Power* unit ends with a transition lesson to provide students with an opportunity to reflect on their mathematical work and group interaction during the unit.

Helping Students Say Good-Bye

When it is time to disband groups that have been working together for some time, it is important to provide opportunities for students to express their feelings and to say good-bye. The transition lessons at the end of each *Number Power* unit are designed for this purpose. You may wish to do some other parting activities, such as:

1. *Group Memories Bulletin Board.* Have groups write favorite memories about their group work or about each other and then post them on a bulletin board labeled "Group Memories."

2. *Group Memory Books.* Have groups make a book that includes work from their favorite investigations, comments from each member about what they liked about the unit and working together with each other, and a picture or drawing of the group.

3. *Thank-You Letters.* Have group members write thank-you letters to each other expressing appreciation for something specific.

4. *Good-bye Celebrations.* Have each group plan a way to celebrate their work together.

(For ideas for parting or closing activities, see Rhodes and McCabe's *The Nurturing Classroom* and Gibbs and Allen's *Tribes*. See Additional Reading, p. 185.)

Number Power Format

The Grade Four *Number Power* Program consists of three units of eight to ten lessons each. These units focus on rational and large numbers and provide opportunities to build on and extend students' understanding of these concepts. In Unit 1, students informally explore and discuss fractions and their uses, and develop an understanding of fractional notation. In Unit 2, students explore part-to-whole relationships and equivalencies, make comparisons, and compute informally with fractions. In Unit 3, students investigate large numbers and build on their understanding of whole numbers. All three units are intended to either supplement or replace existing curricula on these topics.

The Grade Four *Number Power* Program is also designed to help students develop an understanding of and a commitment to the values of fairness, caring, and responsibility. The focus of the first unit is to build on students' previous experience working in groups and to further develop their ability to work together effectively. The second unit focuses on communication skills and helps students analyze the effect of behavior on others and on the group work. The third unit also develops communication skills and emphasizes students taking responsibility for their learning and behavior.

Unit Format

Each unit includes an Overview, a team builder, conceptual lessons, and a transition lesson.
Some units also contain an assessment lesson.

Overview	The Overview will acquaint you with the unit and offer suggestions for implementation. This section provides a synopsis of all the lessons, a discussion of the major mathematical concepts and social understandings that the lessons help students develop, and a list of all the materials you will need for the unit. The Overview also includes a discussion of informal assessment techniques you might use throughout the unit, and a summary of the specific types of student writing opportunities in the unit.
Team-Building Lessons	Each unit begins with a team-building lesson to help group members become acquainted, to begin to develop their sense of unity and group identity, and to develop their group skills.

Assessment Lesson

Unit 3 includes a lesson that provides an opportunity for you to informally assess students' thinking. (Suggestions for ongoing assessment also can be found in each unit Overview and in many of the *Number Power* lessons.) This lesson suggests questions to ask yourself as you observe students, and is intended to give you a sense of the way in which your students approach mathematics, the depth of their thinking and understanding, and the source of their confusions. This lesson also suggests open-ended questions you may pose to students to probe their thinking.

Conceptual Lessons

The lessons that follow the team-building and assessment lessons focus on developing and extending students' sense of number through a variety of cooperative problem-solving experiences. Many of these lessons will take more than one class period. Students use materials such as geoboards, fraction kits, world almanacs, game boards, and calculators to develop their own algorithms and problem-solving strategies, to explore and verify solutions, and to discuss and write about their thinking.

The conceptual lessons also provide opportunities for students to solve problems as a group and to take responsibility for their own behavior and learning. Open-ended questions help students examine their group interaction and the effect of their behavior on their group. The lessons help students to develop fair and responsible ways to work, and to understand the importance of group skills such as sharing the work and materials in a fair way, agreeing before making decisions, and explaining their thinking.

Transition Lessons

Each unit ends with a transition lesson that encourages students to reflect on their mathematical work throughout the unit and to make generalizations and connections. This lesson is also designed to encourage students to think about their group interaction, their successes and problems, and the things they have learned that will help them in future group work.

In addition to this reflection, the transition lesson allows students to express appreciation for each other and to celebrate their work together. After students have worked as a group for a period of time, it may be difficult for them to face separation and move to a new group; the transition lesson gives students a chance to make this break more easily by acknowledging their attachment to their group and providing ways to say good-bye.

Lesson Format

First Page   The first page provides you with the logistical information you need for the lesson.

Notice the lesson summary (A). Next to the summary you will often see an icon (B). This alerts you that something needs your attention prior to the lesson or that the lesson has a special focus: team building, assessment, or transition.

The first page details the dual emphasis of the lesson. It lists the mathematical and social emphases (C and D), as well as the essential mathematical and social concepts the lesson helps develop (E and F). (See Planning, p. xiii, for a discussion about choosing group skills.)

On the first page you will also find a list of the materials specific to the lesson (G) and the suggested group size (H). *The lessons assume that calculators and manipulative materials are available to students at all times to use at their discretion, and that the student materials are available to groups in their work area at the start of the lesson, unless otherwise indicated in a lesson.*

Number Power **Format**

xvii

Interior Pages

Some lessons begin with a section titled "Before the Lesson" (A). This section suggests student activities or material preparation that you may need to undertake prior to the lesson.

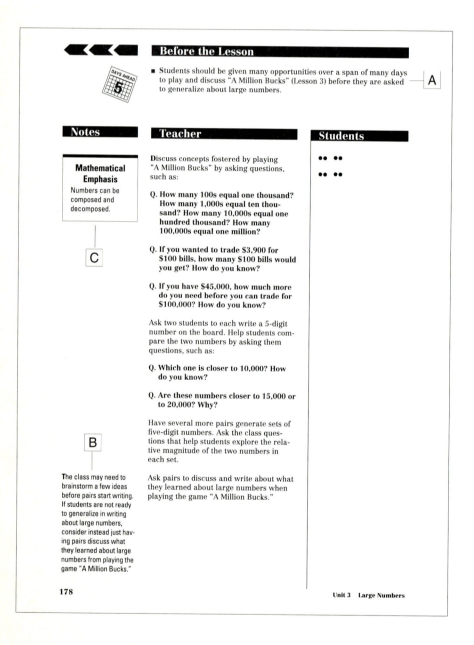

The lesson is divided into three columns. The first column provides notes and suggestions (B) for you. The boxes (C) suggest important mathematical and social concepts as the focus of your open-ended questions in that portion of the lesson.

In some lessons, the first column also contains an assessment icon (D; see next page) accompanied by suggestions for informal assessment.

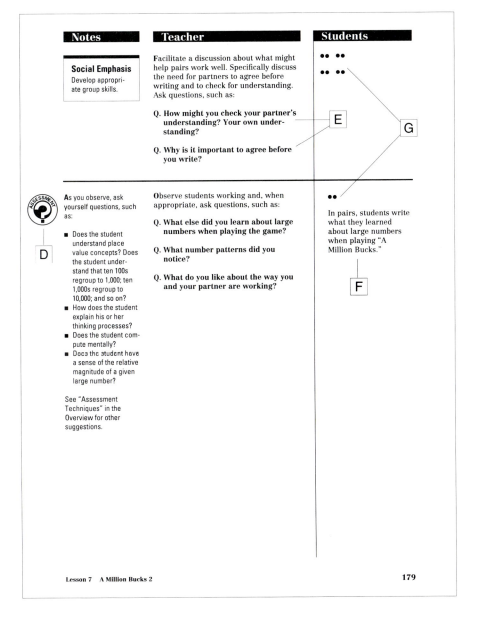

The second column is the lesson plan itself and includes sample open-ended questions to probe and extend your students' thinking (E).

The third column describes the student work (F). It includes icons, described below, that indicate how the students are grouped for each section of the lesson (G).

Group Size Icons

Whole class icons

••••••••••• Teacher talks with the whole class, prior to grouping students, or after group work is complete.

•• ••
•• ••   Teacher talks with the whole class, already in groups of four.

•• ••
•• ••   Teacher talks with the whole class, already in pairs.

Student work icons

••
••   Students work in groups of four.

••   Students work in pairs.

•   Students work individually.

Last Page—Extensions

It seems to be a law of nature that cooperative groups seldom finish their work at the same time. To help manage this and to further students' conceptual development, two additional types of activities are included at the end of each lesson.

The first, "For Pairs [or Groups] That Finish Early" (H), suggests activities for groups to engage in as other groups continue their work. The second, "For the Next Day" (I), further develops concepts or gives students more experience with the same concepts before moving on to the next lesson in the unit. Some of the activities foster students' social, as well as academic, learning.

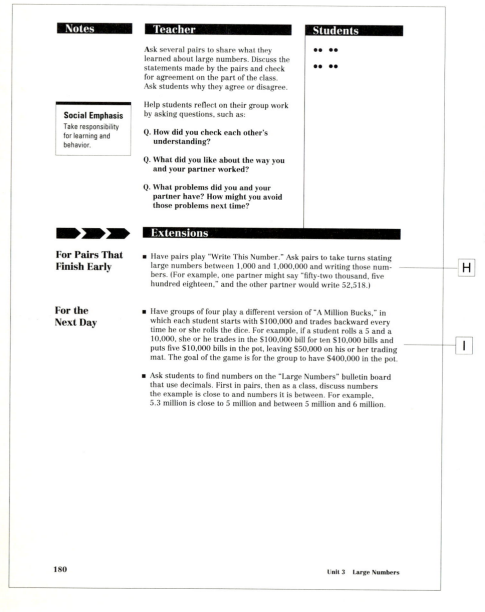

UNIT 1 Overview

Fraction Explorations

Mathematical Development

This unit builds on students' sense of whole numbers and helps them develop their understanding of fractions. The lessons provide opportunities for students to encounter, explore, and discuss fractions and relate them to daily life. Students have informal experiences with fractions as they cook, measure, and investigate shapes on the geoboard. This unit should precede more formal development of fraction concepts.

Lesson 1 is a team builder that sets the stage for the group work. In Lessons 2 and 3, students explore fractions as they adapt recipes. In Lesson 4, students investigate how to divide a set into equal parts. In Lessons 5 and 6, students measure and explore equivalency relationships. In Lessons 7 through 9, students partition shapes and investigate part-to-whole and whole-to-part relationships on a geoboard, and use fractional notation. In Lesson 10, students divide a region into fractional parts and reflect on their work in the unit.

Social Development

The social focus of this unit is to build on students' previous experience working in groups and to help them further develop their group skills, particularly ways to include everyone and share the work. Students are encouraged to reflect on and discuss ways to work effectively and to solve problems. They also have opportunities to analyze the effect of group members' behavior on the group and the group work.

Students should be randomly assigned to groups of four that work together for the entire unit. Groups of four are divided into pairs for Lessons 5, 7, 8, 9, and 10.

Mathematical Emphasis

Conceptually, the experiences in this unit help students construct their understanding that

- Numbers can be used to describe quantities.
- Relationships and equivalencies between quantities can be described.
- A unit or set can be subdivided into equal parts.
- Measurement is approximate. Objects can be measured by making direct comparisons.
- Questions about our world can be asked, and data about those questions can be collected, organized, and analyzed.
- Problems may have more than one solution and may be solved in a variety of ways.
- Once a rule to generate a pattern has been identified, the pattern can usually be extended.
- Equal parts of a whole are not necessarily congruent.
- Geometric figures can be composed of or divided into similar or different shapes.

Social Emphasis

Socially, experiences in this unit help students to

- Develop appropriate group skills.
- Analyze the effect of behavior on others and on the group work.
- Relate the values of fairness, caring, and responsibility to behavior.
- Take responsibility for learning and behavior.

Lessons

This unit includes ten lessons, plus a continuing bulletin board activity. The calendar icon indicates some preparation is needed prior to that lesson.

1. **Team Emblem**
   (page 7)
   Team-building lesson for groups of four that encourages team spirit and cooperation.

2. **Lemonade**
   (page 13)
   Cooking lesson in which groups measure and compute informally, using mixed numbers.

3. **Nutty Cookies!**
   (page 17)
   Cooking lesson in which groups adjust a recipe, measure ingredients, and divide informally.

4. **Sharing Candy Bars**
   (page 23)
   Problem-solving lesson in which groups determine how to divide a set of regions.

5. **Paper Strips**
   (page 29)
   Measurement lesson in which pairs use a nonstandard unit to measure objects and determine how to record the results when an object is smaller or larger than the unit.

6. **Cars and Ramps**
   (page 35)
   Problem-solving lesson in which groups use a nonstandard unit to measure distances, explore equivalencies, and use mixed numbers to record distances.

7. **Geoboards 1**
   (page 41)
   Geoboard lesson in which pairs divide a region into halves and fourths in a variety of ways.

8. **Geoboards 2**
   (page 47)
   Geoboard lesson in which pairs divide a variety of regions into fractional parts.

9. **Geoboards 3**
   (page 55)
   Geoboard lesson in which pairs complete a whole from a given fractional part.

10. **Plant a Garden**
    (page 63)
    Transition lesson in which groups solve a problem by applying what they know about fractions.

"Ways We Use Fractions" Bulletin Board

This ongoing project is woven throughout the unit and requires a large bulletin board. Ask students to collect examples of fractions from newspaper and magazine articles and headlines, recipes, and other sources, and to post these examples on the bulletin board. During the unit, frequently refer to the information in the clippings. Have students discuss such things as when and how fractions are used in daily life, why fractions are necessary, whether they think the fractions on the bulletin board represent estimates or actual numbers, how accurate they think the fractions are, and how they think the fractions might have been derived.

Materials

Throughout the unit, students need access to supplies, such as scissors, pencils, markers, crayons, rulers, and glue sticks. If possible, each group should have a container with these supplies.

The materials needed for the unit are listed below. The first page of each lesson lists the materials specific to that lesson. All blackline masters for transparencies and group record sheets are included at the end of each lesson. Many of the materials are available in the *Number Power* Grade 4 Package.

Teacher Materials

- Overhead projector, markers, and either chart paper or large newsprint
- Large bulletin board
- Pictures of coats of arms (Lesson 1)
- Cooking supplies (Lessons 2 and 3; amounts are based on 32 students, or eight groups of four students each)
  ‣ 2 pounds of sugar
  ‣ 32 ounces of lemon juice concentrate
  ‣ ice (optional)
  ‣ spoons for stirring
  ‣ napkins or paper towels
  ‣ access to water supply and an oven
  ‣ ½ package of yellow or white cake mix per group
  ‣ ¼ cup of vegetable oil per group
  ‣ 1 egg per group
  ‣ ¼ cup of chopped nuts per group
- Transparency of "Nutty Cookies!" group record sheet (Lesson 3)
- Extra paper candy bars made from blackline master (Lesson 4)
- 11" paper strips (Lesson 5; Lesson 6 "Extensions")
- Transparency of "Cars and Ramps" group record sheet (Lesson 6)
- Overhead projector geoboard and geobands (Lessons 7, 8, 9, and 10)
- Transparencies of "Exploring Shapes" group record sheets (Lesson 8)
- "Exploring Shapes: Extensions" group record sheet (Lesson 8 "Extensions")
- Transparencies of "Complete the Whole" group record sheets (Lesson 9)
- "Complete the Whole: Extensions" group record sheets (Lesson 9 "Extensions")
- Transparency of "Geoboard Dot Paper" (Lesson 10)
- Transparency of "Plant a Garden" group record sheet (Lesson 10)

Student Materials

Each pair needs
- Geoboard (Lessons 7, 8, 9, and 10)
- At least 10 geobands or rubber bands (Lessons 7, 8, 9, and 10)
- "Geoboard Dot Paper" (Lessons 7 and 10)
- "Exploring Shapes" group record sheets (Lesson 8)
- "Complete the Whole" group record sheets (Lesson 9)
- "Plant a Garden" group record sheet (Lesson 10)

Each group of four needs
- "Team Emblem" group record sheet (Lesson 1)
- Access to measuring cups and measuring spoons (Lessons 2 and 3)
- 2-quart pitcher and four 10-ounce drinking cups (Lesson 2)
- "Nutty Cookies!" group record sheet (Lesson 3)
- Mixing bowl, spoon, and cookie sheet (Lesson 3)
- At least 7 paper candy bars made from blackline master (Lesson 4)
- 11" paper strip (Lesson 5)
- Five to eight 11" paper strips (Lesson 6)
- 3 or 4 books (Lesson 6)
- Workbook or piece of heavy cardboard for ramp (Lesson 6)
- Small toy car (Lesson 6)
- "Cars and Ramps" group record sheet (Lesson 6)

Teaching Hints

- Prior to each lesson, think about the open-ended questions you might ask to extend or probe students' thinking. Decide which "Extensions" to have ready when groups or pairs finish early. After each lesson, review any "Extensions" students have not explored and decide whether to have them investigate these "Extensions" before going on to the next lesson.

- Encourage students to verbalize their thinking and to explain their thinking in writing.

- You may wish to adapt the recipes in Lessons 2 and 3 if students have dietary restrictions.

- At times, groups may have an odd number of students. In lessons where students are finding equal shares of sets or regions, take advantage of this situation in order to discuss their division strategies and the results.

- Allow students time to explore unfamiliar or infrequently used materials before they use them in the lesson.

- Stress terminology such as *[3] out of [4] equal parts* when describing and when writing about fractions.

Assessment Techniques

This unit helps students develop an understanding of fraction concepts by having them explore real-life situations involving the use of fractions. Their understanding will vary from experience to experience, particularly in the beginning of this process. The assessment techniques suggested in the lessons will help you determine which concepts the students seem to understand and what further experiences they need.

As you observe groups, note students' behavior, as well as their conceptual understanding. (For example, some students might exhibit confidence, while others may give up easily.) Prior to the lesson, prepare possible questions to ask yourself or the students. Be open to students' responses, and probe their thinking by asking follow-up questions that require them to explain further.

Assess Individual Students' Understanding of Fractions

- Before you begin the unit, ask students to write what they know about fractions and about how they have seen fractions used in daily life. Students will have another opportunity to write about what they know about fractions in Unit 2. (See "Before the Lesson" in "Fraction Puzzles," Unit 2, Lesson 1.) Save student explanations in order to help you analyze how students construct, over time, their understanding of fractions. Note that some students, for example, may use fraction terminology but may not understand that ¾, for example, means 3 out of 4 equal parts. Other students may not understand the relationship between equal parts and the whole. For example, students may not understand that ¼ is one of four equal parts and relates to three other equal parts to complete the whole.

Student Writing

Throughout the unit, ask students to verbalize their thinking, and, at times, to explain their thinking in writing. During this unit, students write about

- How they measured distance.
- The relationships and equivalencies between quantities.
- How a region can be subdivided into equal parts.
- A solution to a problem.
- Why they liked working with their partner.

UNIT 1 Fraction Explorations

Lesson 1

Team Emblem

Students create a team name and a team emblem.

Team Builder Emphasis

In this lesson, students

- Get to know each other better.
- Begin to develop an effective working relationship.
- Begin to develop a sense of unity and belonging as a group.

Social Emphasis

In this lesson, students

- Make a plan.
- Include everyone.

Students continue to

- Develop appropriate group skills.

Group Size: 4

Teacher Materials

- Pictures of coats of arms (see "Before the Lesson")

Student Materials

Each group of four needs

- "Team Emblem" group record sheet
- Markers or crayons

Before the Lesson

- Ask students to talk with their families about their names, particularly how they were given their first names and the history of their last names.

- Find examples of coats of arms. (Encyclopedias are a good resource.) Other resources include:
  - Dennys, Rodney. *Heraldry and the Heralds.* Jonathan Cape, 1982.
  - Franklyn, Julian. *Shield and Crest: An Account of the Art and Science of Heraldry.* 3rd ed. Geneological Publishing, 1969.
  - Neubecker, Ottfried. *A Guide to Heraldry.* McGraw, 1979.
  - Puttock, A.G. *A Dictionary of Heraldry and Related Subjects.* Arco, 1986.

Notes

See Forming Groups, page xii, for random-grouping suggestions.

Teacher

As a class, discuss names: why we have names, how we get our names, how we feel about our names, why it is important to know and use people's names.

Randomly assign students to groups of four and state that groups will remain together for the unit as they explore fractions.

Students

Have students talk about their names with each other, discussing questions, such as:

Q. How did you get your first name?

Q. What is the family history of your last name?

Q. Do you like your name? What do you like to be called?

Q. If you could choose a new name, what would it be?

Ask groups to decide on a group name that reflects the names of members of their group.

In groups, students

1. Talk with each other about their names.

2. Decide on a group name that reflects the names of members of their group.

---

8 Unit 1 Fraction Explorations

Notes	Teacher	Students
A cooperative structure such as "Heads Together" (see p. xi) can provide opportunities for all students to be involved in the discussion. **A** system of symbols exists, known as heraldry, that is used to represent individuals, families, countries, and some institutions. The basic heraldic symbol is an emblem called a coat of arms, which first appeared in the early 1100s and was used originally on the shields of knights so that followers could recognize them. Today, the governments of many nations, states, and cities have coats of arms. In the United States, anyone may create and use a coat of arms.	**H**ave groups share their group names. Have students discuss what they think is important for working effectively as a group and list their suggestions on the chalkboard. Explain that groups will make a team emblem that incorporates all their names and their group name. Discuss the history of coats of arms and show examples. Provide each group with a copy of the "Team Emblem" group record sheet. Ask groups to plan what they will put on their emblems and how they will include everyone in the work.	⁛ ⁛ ⁛ ⁛
If groups are having difficulty working, draw their attention to the ideas about working together listed on the chalkboard and ask which ideas might help them.	**O**bserve groups and ask questions, such as: Q. What is your plan? Q. What do you like about how you are working together? Q. How are you making decisions? Q. How are you including everyone in the work?	 In groups, students plan and make a team emblem that includes their individual and team names.

Lesson 1   Team Emblem

Notes	Teacher	Students
	Have groups share their emblems. Discuss questions, such as:	∷ ∷ ∷ ∷
	Q. What did you like about making your emblem?	
Social Emphasis Develop appropriate group skills.	Q. How did you make decisions? Did that work well? Why?	
	Q. What would you do differently the next time you work together?	
See the Overview, p. 2, for suggestions about developing the bulletin board.	Explain that in this unit, the class will explore and discuss fractions. Introduce the class bulletin board, "Ways We Use Fractions." Ask students to ask their families and others how they use fractions and to bring to class examples of fractions from newspapers, magazines, recipes, and other sources.	

Extensions

For Groups That Finish Early

- Have groups decorate their team emblem.

- Have groups compare the number of letters in their first names. Ask questions, such as:

    Q. Are any group members' names about half as long as yours? How do you know?

    Q. What name can you think of that has about half as many letters as your name? How do you know it is half as long as yours?

For the Next Day

- Have groups add to the "Ways We Use Fractions" bulletin board by looking in newspapers, magazines, recipes, and other sources for examples of fractions.

Names

Team Emblem

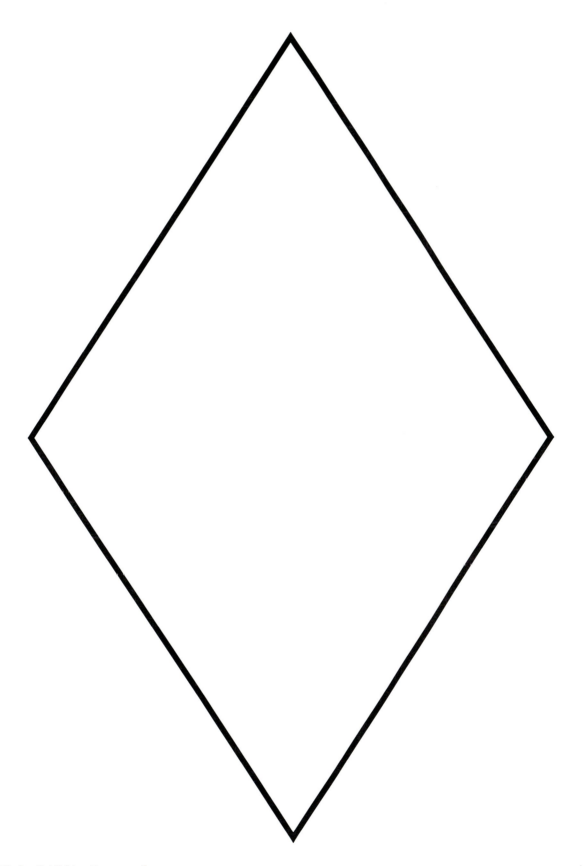

© Addison-Wesley Publishing Company, Inc.

Unit 1, Lesson 1: Team Emblem   Group Record Sheet

UNIT 1 Fraction Explorations

Lesson 2

Lemonade

Students decide how much lemonade to make for their group, adjust the recipe, and make the lemonade. This lesson may take two class periods.

Mathematical Emphasis

In this lesson, students

- Use fractions to adjust a recipe.
- Measure ingredients.

Students add to their understanding that

- Relationships and equivalencies between quantities can be described.
- Numbers can be used to describe quantities.
- Once a rule to generate a pattern has been identified, the pattern can usually be extended.

Social Emphasis

In this lesson, students

- Share the work in a fair way.
- Use materials in a responsible way.

Students continue to

- Develop appropriate group skills.
- Analyze the effect of behavior on others and on the group work.

Group Size: 4

Teacher Materials

- Water
- 32 ounces of lemon juice concentrate
- 2 pounds of sugar
- Ice (optional)
- Spoons for stirring
- Napkins or paper towels

Student Materials

Each group of four needs

- Access to measuring cups and measuring spoons
- 2-quart pitcher
- Four 10-ounce drinking cups
- Paper and pencil

Lesson 2 Lemonade 13

Before the Lesson

- Adapt the lesson according to any dietary restrictions your students may have.

- Ask another adult to assist you during this lesson, if needed.

- Decide how you want to organize the process of making the lemonade. You might adapt one of these suggestions:

  1. Set up several tables around the room and have students rotate to each station as they make their lemonade. For instance, place one table near the source of water; set up two tables for lemon juice, sugar, and measuring utensils; and set up another table where students stir the ingredients and pick up their drinking cups.

  2. Set up one work station per group, including at each station all the ingredients and measuring utensils required to make the lemonade.

  3. Set up a single work station where, one at a time, the groups make their lemonade while the other students work on another activity or subject.

Notes

Teacher

First in groups, then as a class, discuss what students learned about the use of fractions from their interviews with their families and others. Discuss the examples of fractions students brought from newspapers, magazines, recipes, and other sources. Post these on the bulletin board.

Introduce the lesson, explaining that students will make lemonade. Ask questions, such as:

Q. Who has had a lemonade stand?

Q. What materials did you need to make the lemonade?

Q. What decisions did you have to make?

Write this recipe on the chalkboard:

1 ½ tablespoons lemon juice
2 ½ tablespoons sugar
1 cup water
Makes one glass of lemonade.

Students

∷ ∷
∷ ∷

Notes	Teacher	Students
Groups may decide that members may want to drink different amounts of lemonade. **G**roups may need access to measuring cups and spoons to help them decide the amount of each ingredient they will need.	**E**xplain that groups are to decide how many cups of lemonade to make, then decide and record the amount of each ingredient they will need for that quantity.	:: :: :: ::
	As groups work, ask questions, such as: Q. How did you decide how much lemonade to make? Q. How do you know you have the correct proportion of water and lemon juice? Water and sugar?	:: In groups, students 1. Decide how many cups of lemonade to make for their group. 2. Decide and record the amount of each ingredient needed.
You may want the class to brainstorm the tasks involved in making the lemonade, such as: ■ measuring the water ■ measuring the lemon juice ■ measuring the sugar ■ stirring the ingredients ■ pouring the lemonade into cups	**E**xplain the logistics for making the lemonade and that, after tasting their lemonade, students may add more of an ingredient if they wish. Facilitate a discussion about responsible ways to handle the ingredients and utensils and how groups might share the work.	:: :: :: ::
Students will need to estimate ½ tablespoon. Encourage students to estimate and to invent their own ways to find fractional parts of measuring tools.	**H**ave groups make their lemonade. Ask questions, such as: Q. How are you deciding what is ½ tablespoon? Q. How are you sharing the work? Do you think that is a fair way to work? Why?	:: In groups, students make their lemonade.

Lesson 2   Lemonade

Notes	Teacher	Students
	Have groups share their recipes and the strategies they used to determine the proportions. As a class, discuss questions, such as:	:: :: :: ::
	Q. Did you decide to add more of any ingredient to make the lemonade taste the way you like it? How did you decide what else to add?	
	Q. How did you measure ½ tablespoon?	

Mathematical Emphasis
Once a rule to generate a pattern has been identified, the pattern can usually be extended.

Number of Cups	Tbsp. of Lemon Juice	Tbsp. of Sugar
1	1½	2½
2	3	5
3	4½	7½
4	6	10
5		
6		
7		

Social Emphasis
Analyze the effect of behavior on others and on the group work.

First in groups, then as a class, discuss questions, such as:

Q. How much lemon juice and sugar would you need for 2 cups of water? 3 cups of water? 4 cups of water? 5 cups of water? How do you know?

As students report the amounts and list them on a chart (such as the sample on the left), ask:

Q. What patterns and relationships do you notice?

Q. How much lemon juice and sugar do you need for 6 cups of water?

Help students reflect on the group work by asking:

Q. How did your group work? What would you change the next time you work together?

Q. In what ways were group members cooperative? How did that affect your work?

:: ::
:: ::

Extensions

For Groups That Finish Early

- Have groups estimate how much lemonade would be needed for the whole class, compute the amount of each ingredient needed, and write a class lemonade recipe. Have groups post their recipes on the "Ways We Use Fractions" bulletin board.

For the Next Day

- Have groups use the same lemonade recipe (1½ tablespoons of lemon juice per cup of water and 2½ tablespoons of sugar per cup of water) and discuss how much water they would need if they used 7½ tablespoons of lemon juice and 12½ tablespoons of sugar.

UNIT 1 Fraction Explorations

Lesson 3

Nutty Cookies!

Students adjust a recipe for two dozen cookies to make one dozen cookies. They measure the ingredients, bake the cookies, and share them equally. This lesson may take two class periods.

Mathematical Emphasis

In this lesson, students

- Use fractions to adjust a recipe.
- Measure ingredients.

Students add to their understanding that

- A unit or set can be subdivided into equal parts.
- Relationships and equivalencies between quantities can be described.
- Numbers can be used to describe quantities.

Social Emphasis

In this lesson, students

- Make a plan.
- Use materials in a responsible way.
- Include everyone.

Students continue to

- Develop appropriate group skills.
- Relate the values of fairness, caring, and responsibility to behavior.

Group Size: 4

Teacher Materials

- Access to water and oven
- ½ package of yellow or white cake mix per group
- ¼ cup of vegetable oil per group
- 1 egg per group
- ¼ cup of chopped nuts per group
- Napkins or paper towels
- Transparency of "Nutty Cookies!" group record sheet
- Overhead projector and markers

Student Materials

Each group of four needs

- "Nutty Cookies!" group record sheet
- Access to measuring cups and measuring spoons
- Mixing bowl, spoon, and cookie sheet

Lesson 3   Nutty Cookies!

Before the Lesson

- Adapt the lesson according to any dietary restrictions your students may have.

- Ask another adult to assist you during this lesson, if needed.

- Decide how you want to organize the process of making the cookies. See "Lemonade" (Lesson 2) for suggestions on how to set up the classroom.

Notes	Teacher	Students
	Briefly discuss students' experience making lemonade by asking questions, such as:	
	Q. What fractions did you use when you made lemonade?	
	Q. How did you decide how much of each ingredient you needed to make lemonade for your group?	
	Explain that each group will bake one dozen cookies and decide how to share the cookies equally. Ask questions, such as:	
	Q. How many cookies are there in one dozen? Two dozen? ½ dozen? ¼ dozen?	
	Show the "Nutty Cookies!" transparency and discuss the recipe. Ask groups to discuss, agree on, and record the amount of each ingredient needed to make one dozen cookies.	
Mathematical Emphasis A unit or set can be subdivided into equal parts. Groups may need access to measuring cups and spoons as they reduce the recipe.	Observe groups working and, when appropriate, ask questions, such as: Q. How are you computing the amount of each ingredient you need? Can you use the same method for all ingredients? Q. How are you making sure everyone is included?	 In groups, students discuss, decide, and record the amount of each ingredient needed to make one dozen cookies.

18 Unit 1 Fraction Explorations

Notes	Teacher	Students
Some students may compute mentally. Others may use the measuring cups to determine half of the ingredients measured in cups. Stress the informal use of fractions when cooking. Most people compute mentally or informally when doubling or halving the amount of ingredients needed in a recipe. **Nutty Cookies** ½ package cake mix ¼ cup vegetable oil 1 tablespoon water 1 egg ¼ cup nuts Makes one dozen cookies.	Have several groups share their method for finding the amount of each ingredient for one dozen cookies. Ask questions, such as: Q. What method did you use to find the amount of each ingredient? Q. Did any group do it differently? Did you get the same results? Q. What fraction of the original recipe does your new list of ingredients represent? After checking for agreement, write the revised list of ingredients on the transparency. As a class, decide how to divide the cake mix in half. Ask groups to make a plan to include everyone in making the cookies. Have groups mix and bake their cookies, and then decide how to share the cookies equally.	:: :: :: ::
If it does not come up in the discussion, consider asking questions that help students think about responsible ways to handle the utensils and ingredients.	As groups work, ask questions, such as: Q. What will you need to do to make the cookies? Q. How did you decide what each person will do? Q. How are you including everyone?	:: In groups, students 1. Make a plan for making the cookies that includes everyone. 2. Measure and mix the ingredients. 3. Bake the cookies. 4. Decide how to share the cookies equally.

Lesson 3   Nutty Cookies!

Notes	Teacher	Students
Even though the recipe should yield one dozen cookies, the actual number each group makes may vary. This will add richness to the discussion about dividing the cookies.	First in groups, then as a class, discuss questions, such as: Q. How did your plan for making the cookies work? Q. How did you share your cookies? Who did it differently? Q. What fraction of the total number of cookies did each group member get? How do you know? How many cookies is that? Q. If your group baked two dozen cookies and shared them equally, what fraction of the total number of cookies would each group member get? How do you know? How many cookies is that? Q. Compare the results of equally sharing one dozen cookies with the results of sharing two dozen cookies. What do you notice?	:: :: :: ::
Note that groups with an odd number of students will have different results. As a class, discuss the fractional part of the dozen and number of cookies each member received in different size groups. For example, students in groups of three will each receive 4 cookies. Students in groups of five will each receive $2\frac{2}{5}$ cookies.		

Extensions

For Groups That Finish Early

- Ask groups to discuss how much of each ingredient you needed to buy in order for each group to make one dozen Nutty Cookies.

For the Next Day

- Ask groups to compute the amount of each ingredient they would need to make $2\frac{1}{2}$ dozen Nutty Cookies. Ask groups to write about how they decided this, and post their explanations on the "Ways We Use Fractions" bulletin board.

Names

Nutty Cookies!

Recipe for 2 Dozen Cookies

1 package cake mix
½ cup vegetable oil
2 tablespoons water
2 eggs
½ cup nuts

Put all ingredients in a bowl. Stir thoroughly. Use a spoon to drop cookies at least an inch apart on a cookie sheet. Bake cookies at 350 degrees for 10 to 12 minutes.

Recipe for 1 Dozen Cookies

__ package cake mix
__ cup vegetable oil
__ tablespoons water
__ eggs
__ cup nuts

Put all ingredients in a bowl. Stir thoroughly. Use a spoon to drop cookies at least an inch apart on a cookie sheet. Bake cookies at 350 degrees for 10 to 12 minutes.

UNIT 1 Fraction Explorations

Lesson 4

Sharing Candy Bars

Students decide how to equally share seven paper candy bars and discuss the relationship of parts to the whole.

DAYS AHEAD 1

Mathematical Emphasis

In this lesson, students

- Share a set of paper candy bars equally among four people.
- Record each person's share.
- Discuss the relationship of parts to the whole.

Students add to their understanding that

- A unit or set can be subdivided into equal parts.
- Problems may have more than one solution and may be solved in a variety of ways.

Social Emphasis

In this lesson, students

- Share the work in a fair way.
- Agree before making a decision.

Students continue to

- Develop appropriate group skills.
- Analyze the effect of behavior on others and on the group work.
- Relate the values of fairness, caring, and responsibility to behavior.

Teacher Materials

- 2 extra paper candy bars per group (see "Before the Lesson")
- At least 25 extra paper candy bars per group for "Extensions"

Student Materials

Each group of four needs

- Sheet of 18" × 24" newsprint, or other paper, to use as a record sheet
- Scissors
- Glue stick
- Marker
- At least 7 paper candy bars (see "Before the Lesson")

Group Size: 4

Lesson 4 Sharing Candy Bars

Before the Lesson

- Copy and cut apart the paper candy bars (see blackline master). You will need nine paper candy bars per group for the lesson. For "Extensions," you will need at least 25 paper candy bars per group.

Notes	Teacher	Students
A cooperative structure such as "Heads Together" (see p. xi) can provide opportunities for all students to be involved in the discussion.	Introduce the lesson by facilitating a discussion about sharing. Ask questions, such as: Q. **What things might need to be shared in equal amounts?** Q. **How is sharing a football different from sharing a candy bar?**	∷ ∷ ∷ ∷
If groups do not have four members, they may choose to divide the seven candy bars among their number or as if they had four members.	Explain that groups will decide how to equally share seven paper candy bars, cut the paper candy bars into equal portions, glue the portions onto their newsprint record sheet, and record the amount each person received. Facilitate a discussion about why it is important for students to agree before they glue the paper candy bars.	

Observe groups and ask yourself the following questions: Q. How do students show they understand how many equal parts make a whole? Q. Do students try to prove that the parts are equal? How? Q. How do students record the amount each is to receive? Do they use fractional notation?	**O**bserve students, and when appropriate, ask questions, such as: Q. **What is your strategy for dividing the candy bars?** Q. **What have you found out so far? What will you try now?** Q. **How have you recorded each person's share? What does that number mean?** Q. **How are you checking that everyone agrees before gluing?** Q. **How are you sharing the work?**	∷ In groups, students 1. Equally divide the seven paper candy bars. 2. Check for agreement, then glue each portion onto their record sheet. 3. Write a statement about the portion each person received.

Unit 1 Fraction Explorations

Notes	Teacher	Students

Mathematical Emphasis

A unit or set can be subdivided into equal parts.

Help students focus their discussion on how they arrived at their answer. Encourage students to explain their thinking in detail.

Some groups will record each person's share for a group of four as 1¾, while others might say 7/4, or 1 and ½ and ¼, or 1 + ¼ + ¼ + ¼, or 1 + ¾. Ask students to show how these are the same. Help students to connect language such as *[3] out of [4] equal parts* to the symbolic representation [¾]. Students need many experiences and opportunities to discuss the meaning of fractional notation.

Throughout this unit, stress terminology such as *[3] out of [4] equal parts* when describing fractional parts and writing fractions.

Ask groups to explain how they shared the paper candy bars and how they recorded each person's share. Ask questions, such as:

Q. **What was each person's share?** [1 ¾ candy bars for a group of four] **How do you know?**

Q. **If your group has three members, what is each person's share?** [2 ⅓ candy bars] **If your group has five members, what is each person's share?** [1 ⅖ candy bars] **How do you know?**

Q. **If two people in your group put their share of candy bars together, how many candy bars would that be?** [For a group of three, 4 ⅔ candy bars. For a group of four, 3 ½ candy bars. For a group of five, 2 ⅘ candy bars.] **How do you know?**

Provide groups with extra paper candy bars. First in groups, then as a class, discuss questions, such as:

Q. **If a candy bar is cut into four equal parts, how might one of those equal parts be represented using fractional notation?** [¼] **Two of the four equal parts?** [2/4] **Three of the four equal parts?** [¾] **How many fourths make the whole candy bar?** [4/4]

Q. **If a candy bar is cut into thirds, how many thirds make the whole candy bar?** [3] **How do you know? How do we write one out of three equal parts?** [⅓] **Two out of three equal parts?** [⅔]

:: ::
:: ::

Lesson 4 Sharing Candy Bars

| **Notes** | **Teacher** | **Students** |

Social Emphasis
Analyze the effect of behavior on others and on the group work.

Have students reflect on their work together. Ask questions, such as:

Q. How did your group share the work? Do you think that was fair? Why?

Q. What kinds of behavior helped your group? What kinds of behavior caused problems for your group? How did your group handle any problems?

To help students develop their understanding of part-to-whole relationships, have groups investigate the questions in "Extensions" before going on to the next lesson.

Extensions

For Groups That Finish Early

- Provide extra paper candy bars and ask groups to investigate one or more of the following questions and to record their findings:

    1. How much is each person's share when four people equally share 3, 4, 5, 6, 7, 8, 9, or 10 paper candy bars? [$3/4$, 1, $5/4$, $6/4$, $7/4$, 2, $9/4$, and $10/4$, respectively.]

    2. How much is each person's share when five people equally share 4, 5, 6, 7, 8, 9, or 10 paper candy bars? [$4/5$, 1, $6/5$, $7/5$, $8/5$, $9/5$, and 2, respectively.]

    3. What numbers of paper candy bars are easiest to share among four people? [4 and 8] Why?

For the Next Day

- Have students investigate one or more of the activities suggested under "For Groups That Finish Early."

26   Unit 1   Fraction Explorations

Candy Bar	Candy Bar
Candy Bar	Candy Bar
Candy Bar	Candy Bar
Candy Bar	Candy Bar
Candy Bar	Candy Bar

UNIT 1 Fraction Explorations

Lesson 5

Paper Strips

Using a paper strip, students measure objects in the classroom and record the measurements. This lesson may take two class periods.

Mathematical Emphasis

In this lesson, students

- Use a paper strip to measure the length, width, or height of objects.

Students add to their understanding that

- A unit or set can be subdivided into equal parts.
- Measurement is approximate. Objects can be measured by making direct comparisons.
- Relationships and equivalencies between quantities can be described.

Social Emphasis

In this lesson, students

- Help each other stay on task.
- Share the work in a fair way.

Students continue to

- Develop appropriate group skills.
- Take responsibility for learning and behavior.

Group Size: 2

Teacher Materials

- 11″ paper strip (see blackline master)
- Extra 11″ paper strips

Student Materials

Each pair needs

- 11″ paper strip (see blackline master)
- Paper and pencil

Lesson 5   Paper Strips

29

Notes	Teacher	Students
	Divide the groups of four into pairs. Have pairs discuss items on the bulletin board that relate fractions and measurement.	•• •• •• ••
	Show a paper strip, ask pairs to discuss which objects in the classroom they could measure using the paper strip as their unit of measure, then have pairs explain their thinking.	
	Ask pairs to choose objects, measure them with their paper strip, and record the measurements.	
Mathematical Emphasis Measurement is approximate. Objects can be measured by making direct comparisons.	**Observe** pairs and, when appropriate, ask questions, such as: Q. **What do you like about how you are working together?** Q. **Are you helping each other stay on task? How?** Q. **How are you sharing the work? Are you both happy with this? Why?** Q. **How are you deciding which objects to measure?** Q. **Show me how you measured** [the desk]. **What is the length** [width, height]? **How did you write that?**	•• In pairs, students 1. Choose objects to measure. 2. Use one paper strip to measure the length, height, or width of the objects. 3. Record measurements.

Notes

Student responses will vary. Some students may describe the measurements in informal terms; for example, students might say they measured objects that were close to one strip long, or a little longer than half of the strip, or between one and one-half and two strips long.

Stress the approximate nature of measurement by encouraging students to use terms such as *close to*, *about*, *a little more or less than*, and *between* when measuring.

Teacher

Ask several pairs to share their measurements and to demonstrate how they made and recorded these measurements. Discuss questions, such as:

Q. **How did you measure objects longer than a paper strip? How did you record that measurement?**

Q. **How did you determine the length of an object that was shorter than a paper strip? How did you record that measurement?**

Q. **Why do you think pairs had different measurements for the same objects?**

If these ideas do not come out in the class discussion, ask the following questions:

Q. **If you fold this strip in half, how many equal parts do you have? [2] How do you write one out of two equal parts? [1/2]**

Q. **If an object measures close to one and one-half paper strips how do you write that? [1 1/2]**

Q. **If you fold the strip in half again, how many equal parts do you have? [4] How do you write one out of four equal parts? [1/4] Two out of four equal parts? [2/4] What is another name for [2/4]? [1/2] How do you know? Three out of four equal parts? [3/4] Four out of four equal parts? [4/4] What is another name for [4/4]? How do you know?**

Students

•• ••

•• ••

Lesson 5   Paper Strips

Notes	Teacher	Students
A cooperative structure such as "Think, Pair, Share" (see p. xi) can provide opportunities for all students to reflect on a problem and discuss their thinking.	First in pairs, then as a class, discuss the following problem: Max and Rebecca measured the width of a desk and recorded that the width was between 3½ and 4 paper strips. If Max and Rebecca needed to be more precise, what are the possible widths the desk could be? Explain your thinking.	
Social Emphasis Take responsibility for learning and behavior.	Q. How did you and your partner solve this problem? What other strategies did pairs use to solve this problem? Q. When have you estimated measurements? When have you needed to be more precise when measuring? Help students reflect on their group work by discussing questions, such as: Q. What made you proud about the way you and your partner worked? Q. How did you and your partner share the work? Q. Did you have any problems staying on task? If so, what did you do?	

Extensions

For Pairs That Finish Early

- Ask pairs to find and measure objects in the room that they think are longer than two, but shorter than four, paper strips. Record the lengths and names of the objects measured, and post on the "Ways We Use Fractions" bulletin board.

For the Next Day

- Continue with the next lesson, "Cars and Ramps."

UNIT 1 Fraction Explorations

Cars and Ramps

Lesson 6

Students investigate how far a toy car can travel after it goes down a ramp, using paper strips to measure distances. This lesson may take two class periods.

DAYS AHEAD 3

Mathematical Emphasis

In this lesson, students

- Measure distances.
- Organize and interpret data.

Students add to their understanding that

- A unit or set can be subdivided into equal parts.
- Measurement is approximate. Objects can be measured by making direct comparisons.
- Questions about our world can be asked, and data about those questions can be collected, organized, and analyzed.

Social Emphasis

In this lesson, students

- Include everyone.
- Use materials in a responsible way.

Students continue to

- Develop appropriate group skills.
- Relate the values of fairness, caring, and responsibility to behavior.
- Take responsibility for learning and behavior.

Group Size: 4

Teacher Materials

- Overhead projector and markers
- Transparency of "Cars and Ramps" group record sheet
- Paper strips for "Extensions" (see Lesson 5)

Student Materials

Each group of four needs

- Five to eight 11" paper strips (see Lesson 5)
- Paper and pencil
- 3 or 4 books
- Workbook or piece of heavy cardboard for ramp
- Small toy car
- "Cars and Ramps" group record sheet

Lesson 6 Cars and Ramps

Before the Lesson

- Collect toy cars, books, and cardboard for ramps. If no heavy cardboard is available, use two letter-size file folders per ramp or a standard size student workbook. Cut five to eight paper strips for each group using the blackline master. Find space for the trial runs in the hallway, on the classroom floor, or on the playground. (Toy cars will not travel far on a carpeted surface.)

Notes | Teacher | Students

In a central location, build a ramp with several books and a sheet of cardboard. Have the class gather around the ramp. Show a paper strip (from "Paper Strips," Lesson 5) and a toy car. Ask students to speculate how far (using paper strips as their unit of measure) the toy car might travel after it goes down the ramp.

Explain that groups will experiment with how far they can make a toy car travel after it goes down a ramp. State that groups will make two trial runs, measure the distance with paper strips, and record their measurements.

Social Emphasis
Relate the values of fairness, caring, and responsibility to behavior.

Facilitate a discussion about ways groups might work well together by asking questions, such as:

Q. What can you do to make sure everyone is included in the work? Why is this important?

Q. What could you do or say if you feel you are being left out? How is that being responsible?

Q. What are responsible ways to handle the materials?

Observe groups and, when appropriate, ask questions, such as:

Q. What have you found out so far?

Q. How are you recording the distances the car traveled?

Q. How are you measuring the distance if the car curves?

Q. How is everyone participating?

In groups, students

1. Build a ramp.

2. Make two trial runs and measure and record the distance of each run.

Unit 1 Fraction Explorations

Notes	Teacher	Students
Student responses will vary. Some groups may record the measurements in informal terms. For example, groups might record that the distance is a little longer than two paper strips or between two and three paper strips. Others may measure the distance by folding the paper strips into four equal parts and estimate the distance to the nearest fourth. Some might fold the paper strips into smaller fractional parts. Ask questions, such as: **Q.** If you were measuring with a strip divided into eight equal parts, how would you write one out of eight equal parts? [⅛] Two out of eight equal parts? [²⁄₈], and so on.	**H**ave several groups share their results with the class. Facilitate a discussion about measuring when the distance is less than one paper strip or more than one paper strip. Have students model for each other how their group measured. Show the "Cars and Ramps" transparency. Explain that groups will experiment with how far they can make their toy car travel by making three more trial runs, measuring and recording the distance their car travels, and writing about how they measured.	∷ ∷ ∷ ∷
	Observe groups and, when appropriate, ask questions, such as: Q. What did you expect would happen? Q. What have you found out so far? Are you surprised? Q. What changes are you making in the design of your ramp? Q. How are you recording the distance?	∷ In groups, students 1. Make three trial runs and measure and record the distance of each run. 2. Write about their furthest trial run and how they measured the distance.
Mathematical Emphasis Questions about our world can be asked, and data about those questions can be collected, organized, and analyzed.	**H**ave groups report the distance their car traveled for the farthest trial run and list these distances on the board. Ask questions, such as: Q. What do you notice about these results? Q. What do you think caused some cars to travel farther than others?	∷ ∷ ∷ ∷

Lesson 6   Cars and Ramps

| **Notes** | **Teacher** | **Students** |

You may need to discuss what it means to hypothesize.

Ask groups to make a hypothesis about what makes some cars go farther than others and to design one or more experiments to test their hypothesis.

In groups, students

1. Make a hypothesis about factors that affect the distance a toy car travels.

2. Design experiments and test their hypothesis.

Encourage groups to explain the factors they discovered that affect the distance a toy car will travel. Some of these variables might include the ramp's slant and height, the toy car's size and condition, and the floor and ramp surfaces.

Facilitate a class discussion about the groups' experiments by asking questions, such as:

Q. **What was your hypothesis? Did your experiment prove your hypothesis? How or why not?**

Q. **What factors do you think make a difference in the distance a car travels after it goes down a ramp?**

Help students reflect on their group work by asking questions, such as:

Q. **Did everyone in your group feel included? If not, how did they explain how they were feeling?**

Q. **Think to yourself. What did you do to help your group? What did you do to add to your learning?**

Q. **What might you do differently next time you work together?**

Social Emphasis
Take responsibility for learning and behavior.

For Groups That Finish Early

For the Next Day

Extensions

- Ask groups to hypothesize if it is possible to build a ramp that will allow a toy car to travel about ten paper strips, how it might be done, and then to test their hypothesis.

- Have groups contribute to the "Ways We Use Fractions" bulletin board by looking in newspapers, magazines, recipes, and other sources for examples of fractions. Have groups discuss the meaning of the fractions posted on the bulletin board.

Names _____

Cars and Ramps
Directions

Experiment with ramps to find out how far you can make your toy car travel. Make three trial runs, and record the distance of each run. Redesign the ramp after each trial, if you would like to.

Write about your furthest trial run and how you measured the distance your car traveled.

UNIT 1 Fraction Explorations
Geoboards 1

Lesson 7

Students use geoboards to explore how to divide a variety of regions into fractional parts.

Mathematical Emphasis

In this lesson, students

- Divide a region into equal parts.
- Use fractional notation to name equal parts.

Students add to their understanding that

- A unit or set can be subdivided into equal parts.
- Equal parts of a whole are not necessarily congruent.
- Relationships and equivalencies between quantities can be described.
- A problem may have more than one solution and may be solved in a variety of ways.
- Geometric figures can be composed of or divided into similar or different shapes.

Social Emphasis

In this lesson, students

- Share materials in a fair way.
- Share the work in a fair way.
- Use materials in a responsible way.

Students continue to

- Develop appropriate group skills.
- Relate the values of fairness, caring, and responsibility to behavior.

Group Size: 2

Teacher Materials

- Overhead projector
- Geoboard and geobands for the overhead projector

Student Materials

Each pair needs

- Geoboard
- At least 10 geobands or rubber bands
- Pencil
- "Geoboard Dot Paper" group record sheet

Lesson 7 Geoboards 1

41

Before the Lesson

- If students' previous experience with the geoboard has been limited, provide opportunities for them to individually explore the geoboard.

Notes	Teacher	Students
All the shapes students explore in the three geoboard lessons are polygons. A *polygon* is a closed figure consisting of three or more sides. The sides must meet but never cross each other. This is a polygon: This is not a polygon: You may wish to use the term *polygon* instead of *shape* after you have discussed the term with the class.	**D**ivide the groups into pairs and explain that these pairs will work together for the remaining lessons in this unit. Explain that in the next several lessons, pairs will use geoboards to explore fractions. Make a square by putting a geoband around the outside pegs of an overhead projector geoboard, and ask pairs to do the same with their geoboards. Explain that the area inside the geoband is the region students will use for the following two investigations. Ask pairs to find ways to divide the square on the geoboard into two parts that have the same area. Ask questions, such as: Q. What does the term *area* mean? Q. How might you determine if shapes have the same area? Q. What are some fair ways to share materials? Q. What are responsible ways to use the materials?	•• •• •• ••
There are many ways to divide the shape into two parts that have the same area, such as: 	**O**bserve students as they investigate. Ask questions, such as: Q. How do you know the two shapes have the same area? Q. Is there another way to divide the square? Explain.	•• In pairs, students explore ways to divide the square on the geoboard into two parts that have the same area.
	Have pairs show their geoboard solutions on the overhead projector geoboard. Ask questions, such as: Q. How do you know the two shapes have the same area? Is there another way to explain that the areas are the same?	•• •• •• ••

Notes	Teacher	Students
	Q. What fraction describes one of the two parts? How can we write that? What fraction describes two of the two parts? How can we write that? What does that equal?	•• •• •• ••
	Ask the pairs to explore ways to divide the square on the geoboard into four parts that have the same area and to record their solutions on the "Geoboard Dot Paper."	
Encourage students to explore making different shapes while dividing the geoboard, to discuss how they made the shapes equal in area, and to discuss what the shapes have in common.	**O**bserve students, and when appropriate, ask questions, such as: **Q. How do you know the parts have the same area?** **Q. How would you describe the shapes you have made?** **Q. What do you notice about the shapes you have made?** [For example, two triangles can make a square.] **Q. What do you like about how you are working together?** **Q. How are you sharing the materials?**	•• In pairs, students 1. Explore ways to divide the square on the geoboard into four parts that have the same area. 2. Record solutions on the "Geoboard Dot Paper."
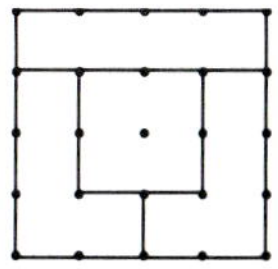	**A**s a class, discuss: **Q. What is one way to divide the square on the geoboard into four parts that have the same area? What are other ways?** Explain that mathematicians use the word *congruent* to describe figures with the same area and shape. Ask students to show solutions they found that have congruent pieces. Make the figure on the left and ask: **Q. What if I divide the board into four equal pieces like this? Do these four pieces have the same area? How do you know?** Have students show solutions they found that have pieces that are not congruent.	•• •• •• ••

Lesson 7   Geoboards 1   43

Notes	Teacher	Students
	Ask students to find other ways to divide the geoboard into four parts that have the same area but are not all the same shape and record their solutions on the "Geoboard Dot Paper."	•• •• •• ••
As you observe students, ask yourself questions, such as: **Q.** How do students verify that parts have the same area? **Q.** Are students able to find more than one solution to the problem?	**O**bserve students and ask questions, such as: **Q.** How can you verify that the four parts have the same area? **Q.** What do you know about the shapes you have made? **Q.** How are you sharing the work? Is this way agreeable to you both? If not, what would you do differently?	•• In pairs, students 1. Explore other ways to divide the square on the geoboard into four parts that have the same area but are not all the same shape. 2. Record their solutions.
Social Emphasis Relate the values of fairness, caring, and responsibility to behavior.	Have pairs show their solutions on the overhead projector geoboard. Ask questions, such as: **Q.** What is something you found out from exploring with the geoboard? **Q.** What fraction describes one of the four parts? Explain. **Q.** Do three of the four parts represent more or less than ½ of the square? How do you know? **Q.** Think to yourself: In what ways did I work responsibly?	•• •• •• ••

Extensions

For Pairs That Finish Early

- Ask pairs to create a different shape on the geoboard, divide it into four parts that have the same area, and describe one of the parts using a fraction.

- Ask pairs to create a shape on the geoboard, divide it into three parts that have the same area, and describe one of the parts using a fraction.

For the Next Day

- Continue with the next lesson, "Geoboards 2."

Geoboard Dot Paper

UNIT 1 Fraction Explorations

Lesson 8

Geoboards 2

Students find equal parts of a whole, using geoboards to explore how to divide different regions into fractional parts. This lesson make take two class periods.

Mathematical Emphasis

In this lesson, students

- Divide a region into equal parts.
- Use fractional notation to name equal parts.

Students add to their understanding that

- A unit or set can be subdivided into equal parts.
- Equal parts of a whole are not necessarily congruent.
- Relationships and equivalencies between quantities can be described.
- A problem may have more than one solution and may be solved in a variety of ways.
- Geometric figures can be composed of or divided into similar or different shapes.

Social Emphasis

In this lesson, students

- Share the materials in a fair way.
- Share the work in a fair way.
- Disagree in a kind way.

Students continue to

- Develop appropriate group skills.
- Relate the values of fairness, caring, and responsibility to behavior.

Group Size: 2

Teacher Materials

- Overhead projector and markers
- Geoboard and geobands for the overhead projector
- Transparencies of "Exploring Shapes" group record sheets
- "Exploring Shapes: Extensions" group record sheets for "Extensions"

Student Materials

Each pair needs

- Geoboard
- At least 10 geobands or rubber bands
- Pencil
- "Exploring Shapes" group record sheets

Lesson 8 Geoboards 2

Notes	Teacher	Students
	As a class, discuss the "Geoboards 1" lesson and what students learned about shapes and fractions.	•• •• •• ••
	Explain that pairs will continue to divide shapes into parts that have the same area.	
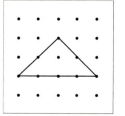 **Social Emphasis** Relate the values of fairness, caring, and responsibility to behavior.	Make the closed figure to the left on the overhead projector geoboard. Ask pairs to make the figure on their geoboards, to divide it into four parts having the same area, and then to share how they divided the shape with another pair. Ask questions, such as: Q. **How might you and your partner share the work?** Q. **What might you say if you do not agree with the other pairs' ideas? What do you think is important to remember when you disagree with someone?**	
Encourage students to persevere with this exploration. There are many ways to divide the figure into four parts that have the same area, such as: 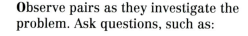 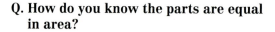	**O**bserve pairs as they investigate the problem. Ask questions, such as: Q. **How do you know the parts are equal in area?** Q. **Are three of the parts more or less than half of the shape? How do you know?** Q. **What fraction describes one of the four parts? Explain your thinking. What fraction describes three of the four parts? Explain your thinking.** Q. **How would you describe the shapes you have made?** Q. **How can different shapes have the same area?** Q. **What shapes make the whole?** [For example, 4 triangles can make a larger triangle.] Q. **What do you like about how you and your partner are working? How is your group working?**	•• In pairs, students 1. Explore ways to divide the shape into four parts that have the same area. 2. Share how they divided the shape with another pair.

Unit 1 Fraction Explorations

Notes	Teacher	Students
	Show the first "Exploring Shapes" transparency on the overhead projector and discuss the directions. Hand out the "Exploring Shapes" group record sheets.	•• •• •• ••
If students have trouble cooperating with each other, help them analyze the effect of the behaviors that are causing difficulty by posing open-ended questions, such as: Q. What seems to be causing problems? Q. What could you do about that? Q. How might that help? How is that fair?	**O**bserve pairs and, when appropriate, ask questions, such as: Q. **How are you sharing the work? Do you both think that it is fair? Why?** Q. **How are you sharing the materials? Do you both think that is fair? Why?** Q. **How can you prove the parts are equal in area?** Q. **Are the parts congruent? How do you know?**	•• In pairs, students 1. Make each shape on the geoboard. 2. Find several ways to divide each shape into parts that have the same area. 3. Draw one of their solutions on their group record sheet, describe how the shape was divided, and answer the question.
Mathematical Emphasis A unit or set can be subdivided into equal parts. **A**s students compare how the initial shapes have been divided, encourage them to describe the shapes made as a result of the division process and to explain how to make the shapes.	As a class, discuss the investigations. Have three pairs with different solutions show their geoboards. Ask questions, such as: Q. **What do you notice about the ways the shape was divided?** Q. **What is the same about these three solutions?** Q. **What is different about all these solutions?** Q. **What fraction describes one of the parts in this shape?** (Point to one of the geoboards.) **How is that different from or the same as this fractional part?** (Point to another geoboard.) Q. **How many parts are needed to make more than ½ of this shape?** (Point to a geoboard.) **How does that compare to how many parts are needed to make more than one-half of this shape?** (Point to another geoboard.) Q. **How many equal parts make the whole?** (Point to a geoboard.) **How can that be written?**	•• •• •• ••

Lesson 8   Geoboards 2

Notes	Teacher	Students
	Q. How many equal parts make half of this shape? (Point to a geoboard.) How can that be written? (Repeat these questions for the other two geoboards.)	•• •• •• ••
	Repeat the process for the second investigation.	
	To help students reflect on their work together, ask questions, such as:	
Social Emphasis Relate the values of fairness, caring, and responsibility to behavior.	Q. What compliments would you give yourself today about how you worked? Q. How did you and your partner work in a responsible way? Did that help your work? How? Q. What compliments would you give the other pair about how they worked with you?	

Extensions

For Pairs That Finish Early

- Have pairs investigate the problems on the "Exploring Shapes: Extensions" group record sheet.

- Ask pairs to create a shape on the geoboard and divide it into four parts that have the same area but are not all the same shape.

For the Next Day

- Have pairs investigate the problems on the "Exploring Shapes: Extensions" group record sheet, if they have not already done so.

- Have students contribute to the "Ways We Use Fractions" bulletin board by looking in newspapers, magazines, recipes, and other sources for examples of fractions. Have pairs discuss the meaning of the fractions posted on the bulletin board.

- Continue with the next lesson, "Geoboards 3."

Names
_____

Exploring Shapes

Make each shape on your geoboard. Divide each shape into parts that have the same area.

1. Write about how you divided the shape.

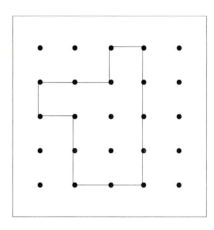

- What fraction describes one of the parts?_____

2. Write about how you divided the shape.

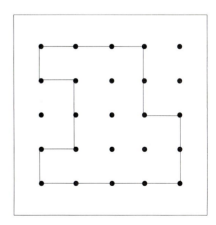

- What fraction describes one of the parts?_____

© Addison-Wesley Publishing Company, Inc.   Unit 1, Lesson 8: Geoboards 2   Group Record Sheet

Make each of these shapes on your geoboard. Divide each shape into parts that have the same area. Draw your solution, describe how you divided the shape, and answer the question.

3. Write about how you divided the shape.

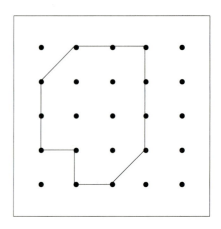

- What fraction describes one of the parts?_____

4. Write about how you divided the shape.

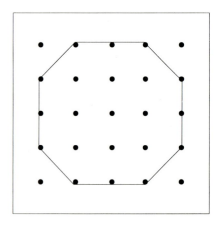

- What fraction describes one of the parts?_____

Unit 1, Lesson 8: Geoboards 2   Group Record Sheet   © Addison-Wesley Publishing Company, Inc.

Names
_____

Exploring Shapes
Extensions

Make each of these shapes on your geoboard. Divide the shape as directed. Draw your solution and answer the questions.

1. Divide the shape into **nine** parts that have the same area.

    • What fraction describes one of the nine equal parts?_____

    • What fraction describes three of the nine equal parts?_____

    • What fraction describes nine of the nine equal parts?_____

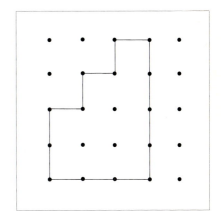

2. Divide the shape into **three** parts that have the same area.

    • What fraction describes one of the three equal parts?_____

    • What is another name for ⅓ of the shape?_____ Explain your thinking.

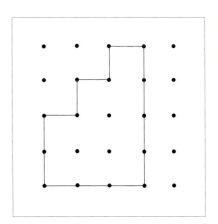

© Addison-Wesley Publishing Company, Inc.   Unit 1, Lesson 8: Geoboards 2 Group Record Sheet

UNIT 1 Fraction Explorations

Lesson 9

Geoboards 3

Students find several solutions to a problem. They make a fractional part of a whole on a geoboard and then find many examples of the whole. This lesson may take two class periods.

Mathematical Emphasis

In this lesson, students

- Find several solutions to a problem.
- Use fractional parts to make a whole.

Students add to their understanding that

- Relationships and equivalencies between quantities can be described.
- A unit or set can be subdivided into equal parts.
- A problem may have more than one solution and may be solved in a variety of ways.
- Geometric figures can be composed of or divided into similar or different shapes.

Social Emphasis

In this lesson, students

- Share materials in a fair way.
- Share the work in a fair way.

Students continue to

- Develop appropriate group skills.
- Relate the values of fairness, caring, and responsibility to behavior.

Group Size: 2

Teacher Materials

- Overhead projector and markers
- Geoboard and geobands for the overhead projector
- Transparencies of "Complete the Whole" group record sheets
- "Complete the Whole: Extensions" group record sheets for "Extensions"

Student Materials

Each pair needs

- Geoboard
- At least 10 geobands or rubber bands
- Pencil
- "Complete the Whole" group record sheets

Lesson 9   Geoboards 3

55

Notes	Teacher	Students
	Have students discuss their experiences with the geoboard in the previous lessons. Briefly explain that pairs will use a geoboard to make a whole shape from a fractional part of a shape. Show the following figure on the overhead projector geoboard: Ask: Q. If this shape represents ½ of the whole, how might the whole look? How many different ways can you make the whole?	•• •• •• ••
	Observe as pairs find several ways to make the whole. Ask questions, such as: Q. Is there another way the whole could look? How might you prove it is the whole?	•• In pairs, students discuss the question and find several ways to make the whole.
Mathematical Emphasis A problem may have more than one solution and may be solved in a variety of ways.	Have pairs share their solutions. Ask questions, such as: Q. How might the whole look? How do you know it is the whole? How else might the whole look? Q. How many parts that are equal in area do you need to make the whole? How do you know? Q. How would you describe the shape you have made? How did you decide what shape to make? Q. How would you explain to someone how to make the shape? Q. What else do you notice about the shape?	•• •• •• ••

56 Unit 1 Fraction Explorations

Notes	Teacher	Students
	Show the "Complete the Whole" transparency, and discuss the directions. Facilitate a discussion about fair and responsible ways to work by asking questions, such as: Q. How did you work in responsible ways in the last geoboard lesson? Q. How did you share the work in the last geoboard lesson? Q. Why is it important to share the work? Hand out the "Complete the Whole" group record sheets.	•• •• •• ••
	Observe pairs and, when appropriate, ask questions, such as: Q. How do you know that is the whole shape? Q. How else might the whole look? Q. How many parts that are equal in area make the whole? Why? Q. What do you know about the shape you have made? Q. How are you sharing the work? Q. How are you sharing the materials?	•• In pairs, students explore the questions on the "Complete the Whole" group record sheets.
Mathematical Emphasis A unit or set can be subdivided into equal parts.	First in pairs, and then as a class, discuss questions, such as: Q. Which figure did you find the most challenging? Why? Q. What did you decide the whole might look like for the [first, second, third, etc.] figure? Is there another way it could look?	•• •• •• ••

Lesson 9   Geoboards 3

| **Notes** | **Teacher** | **Students** |

Show the following shape on the overhead projector geoboard:

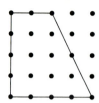

First in pairs, and then as a class, have students discuss questions, such as:

Q. If this shape represents one whole, how might ⅓ of the shape look? How do you know?

Q. Is there another way to represent ⅓ of this shape?

Q. How might ⅔ of the shape look? How do you know?

Have students discuss how they worked in fair and responsible ways by asking questions, such as:

Q. How did you share the work? Was that fair? Why?

Q. What would you say to students who are just beginning to work with geoboards about how to handle the materials?

Q. How did you handle any disagreements?

Social Emphasis
Relate the values of fairness, caring, and responsibility to behavior.

Extensions

For Pairs That Finish Early

- Have one partner create a shape on the geoboard and tell the other partner what fractional part of the whole it represents. Have the second partner create the whole on the geoboard. Then have partners switch roles.

For the Next Day

- Have pairs explore the questions on the "Complete the Whole: Extensions" group record sheet.

Unit 1 Fraction Explorations

Names

Complete the Whole

Make each of these shapes on your geoboard and find as many different ways as you can to make the whole figure. Draw two of your solutions below and be prepared to explain how you know each solution is a whole.

1.

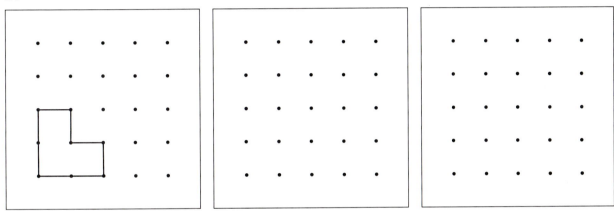

This is ½ of a whole shape.

2.

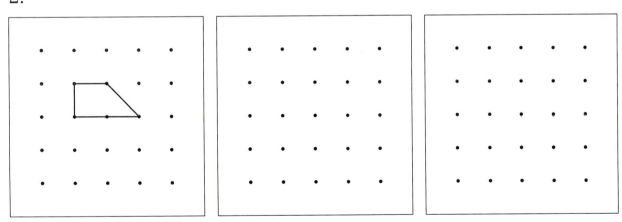

This is ⅓ of a whole shape.

© Addison-Wesley Publishing Company, Inc.   Unit 1, Lesson 9: Geoboards 3   Group Record Sheet

3.

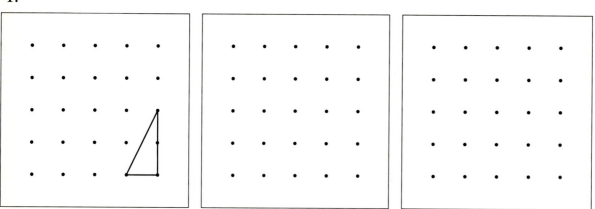

This is ²/₄ of a whole shape.

4.

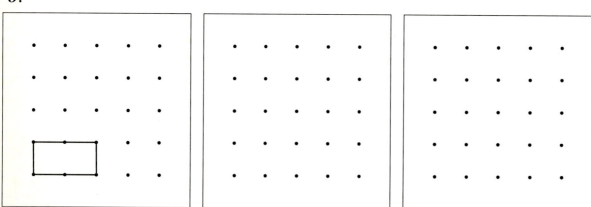

This is ⅛ of a whole shape.

5.

This is ⅓ of a whole shape.

Names

Complete the Whole
Extensions

Make each of these shapes on your geoboard and find as many different ways as you can to make the whole figure. Draw two of your solutions below and be prepared to explain how you know each solution is a whole.

1.

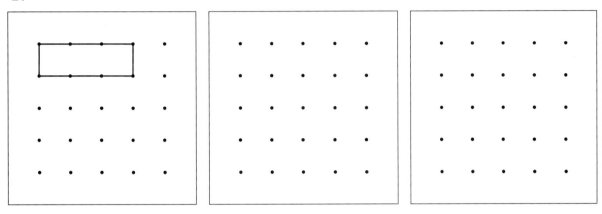

This is 3/8 of a whole shape.

2.

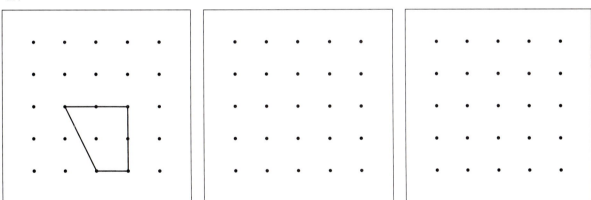

This is 3/4 of a whole shape.

© Addison-Wesley Publishing Company, Inc. Unit 1, Lesson 9: Geoboards 3 Group Record Sheet

UNIT 1 Fraction Explorations

Lesson 10

Plant a Garden

Students design a garden by applying what they know about dividing a region into fractional parts. This lesson may take two class periods.

Transition Emphasis

In this lesson, students

- Add to their understanding that a unit or set can be subdivided into equal parts.
- Add to their understanding that problems may have more than one solution and may be solved in a variety of ways.
- Reflect on how they worked together.
- Thank each other for their work together.

Social Emphasis

In this lesson, students

- Explain their thinking.
- Check for understanding.

Students continue to

- Develop appropriate group skills.
- Analyze the effect of behavior on others and on the group work.

Group Size: 2

Teacher Materials

- Overhead projector
- Geoboard and geobands for the overhead projector
- Transparency of "Plant a Garden" group record sheet
- Transparency of "Geoboard Dot Paper" (see Lesson 7)

Student Materials

Each pair needs

- "Plant a Garden" group record sheet
- Geoboard
- At least 10 Geobands or rubber bands
- "Geoboard Dot Paper" (see Lesson 7)
- Paper and pencil

Notes	Teacher	Students
A cooperative structure such as "Turn to Your Partner" (see p. xi) can provide opportunities for all students to be involved in the discussion.	Introduce the lesson by directing students' attention to the "Ways We Use Fractions" bulletin board. Ask questions, such as:	•• •• •• ••
	Q. How have you used fractions during this unit?	
Mathematical Emphasis Numbers can be used to describe quantities.	Q. What do the items on the bulletin board tell you about how fractions are used in daily life?	
	Q. How might you explain fractions to someone else?	
	Explain that pairs will use fractions to design a garden on a geoboard. Show the "Plant a Garden" transparency and discuss the following:	
	Shaila and Michael got a summer job planting Mr. Garcia's flower garden. Mr. Garcia showed them his square plot of land and said he wanted tulips, daisies, and roses planted in his garden. He asked Shaila and Michael to plant less than half the garden with tulips, to plant twice as much of the area with daisies as tulips, and to plant roses in the rest of the garden. How might Michael and Shaila divide the square plot of land?	
A cooperative structure such as "Think, Pair, Share" (see p. xi) can provide opportunities for all students to reflect on a problem and discuss their thinking.	First individually, then in pairs, ask students to think about and discuss the problem. Ask questions, such as:	•• First individually, and then in pairs, students think about and discuss the problem.
	Q. What problem must Shaila and Michael solve?	
	Q. What information is included in the problem? What information is not included in the problem?	
	Q. What decisions do you need to make?	

	Notes	**Teacher**	**Students**
		Ask students to suggest ways pairs might make decisions about how to plant their garden. Ask questions, such as:	•• •• •• ••
		Q. What does it mean to explain your thinking? Why might this be important to helping your work?	
		Q. How can you check to be sure you understand your partner's ideas?	
		Show the overhead projector geoboard and put a geoband around the outside pegs. Explain that pairs will make a similar square on their geoboard to represent Mr. Garcia's garden.	
		Ask pairs to experiment with solutions, copy one or more solutions onto the "Geoboard Dot Paper," choose one of their solutions and write about how they developed their plan for the garden and why they think Mr. Garcia will be happy with it.	
	As you observe students, ask yourself questions, such as: Q. What strategies do students use to solve the problem? Can they describe those strategies? Q. Do students persist? Q. Are they able to see that there are several solutions to this problem? Q. Do they have a sense of the relationship of parts to the whole? Q. Do they have a sense of fractions that are less than ½? Greater than ½? Students' written explanations also will be helpful as an assessment tool.	Observe pairs and, when appropriate, ask questions, such as: Q. What do you know about this problem? How might that help you solve the problem? Q. How do you know this solution is reasonable? Q. What other solutions might you find for this problem? Q. How are you making sure you understand your partner's thinking? Q. Why do you think this is a good plan for Shaila and Michael?	•• In pairs, students 1. Explore solutions to the problem. 2. Copy one or more solutions onto the "Geoboard Dot Paper." 3. Choose one of their solutions and write about how they developed their plan to the garden and why they think Mr. Garcia will be happy with it.

Lesson 10   Plant a Garden

Notes

Student designs for the garden will vary. Some solutions are as follows:

Tulips = 1/8; Daisies = 1/4; Roses = 5/8

Tulips = 1/4; Daisies = 1/2; Roses = 1/4

Tulips = 1/16; Daisies = 2/16; Roses = 13/16

There are many solutions using sixteenths. Encourage students to find different solutions using sixteenths. List the students' solutions on the chalkboard. For example:

Tulips	Daisies	Roses
1/16	2/16	13/16
2/16	4/16	10/16
3/16	6/16	7/16

Have pairs discuss the number patterns and relationships.

Teacher

Have pairs demonstrate solutions on the overhead projector geoboard. As pairs share solutions, encourage other students to ask them questions. Discuss questions, such as:

Q. What is your plan for the garden? What helped you solve the problem? What other solutions are there?

Q. How do you know your plan fits what Mr. Garcia wanted?

Q. How did you use your knowledge of fractions to solve this problem?

Q. What possible fractional parts of the garden might be planted with roses?

First in pairs, then as a class, reflect on the unit by asking questions such as:

Q. What did you like about working together?

Q. What would you tell a new group that would help them work effectively?

Have pairs decide how to thank each other for their work together and how to say good-bye.

Students

•• ••

•• ••

For Pairs That Finish Early

Extensions

- Ask pairs to choose one activity from the unit that they enjoyed doing together and write about why they liked working on that activity together.

Unit 1   Fraction Explorations

Names _____

Plant a Garden

1. On your geoboard, find solutions to the following problem:

    Shaila and Michael got a summer job planting Mr. Garcia's flower garden. Mr. Garcia showed them his square plot of land and said he wanted tulips, daisies, and roses planted in his garden. He asked Shaila and Michael to plant less than half the garden with tulips, to plant twice as much area with daisies as tulips, and to plant roses in the rest of the garden. How might Shaila and Michael divide the square plot of land?

2. Copy your solutions onto the "Geoboard Dot Paper."

3. Choose one of your solutions and write about how you developed your plan and why you think Mr. Garcia will be happy with it.

UNIT 2 Overview

Fractions: Parts and Wholes

Mathematical Development

This unit provides opportunities for students to think and reason as they construct their understanding of fractions. Using spinners, fractions kits, rulers, data sets, and magazine advertisements, students explore fractions and build on the concepts they developed in the "Fraction Explorations" Unit.

Lesson 1 is a team builder that helps students learn about nonverbal communication. In Lesson 2, students estimate fractional parts of a region. In Lessons 3–6, students investigate the relationship between parts and wholes, compare and order fractions, and explore equivalent relationships. In Lessons 7–9, students measure, collect, and organize data, explore fractional parts of a set, and investigate equivalent fractions. In Lesson 10, students apply what they know about fractions to solve and write problems and to reflect on their work in the unit.

Social Development

The focus of this unit is to provide opportunities for students to analyze how their behavior and the behavior of others affects the group work and interaction. The unit fosters communication skills such as listening, disagreeing in a kind way, and explaining thinking. Open-ended questions help students begin to examine how the underlying values of fairness, caring, and responsibility relate to behavior and how their behavior affects group work and interaction.

Students work in randomly formed groups that stay together throughout the unit; in Lessons 2, 4, 5, 6, 9, and 10 students within each group work in pairs.

Mathematical Emphasis

Conceptually, the experiences in this unit help students construct their understanding that

- Equal parts of a whole are not necessarily congruent.
- A unit or set can be subdivided into equal parts.
- Relationships and equivalencies between quantities can be described.
- Numbers can be used to describe quantities.
- The relative magnitude of numbers can be described.
- Making a reasonable estimate requires gathering and using information.
- Questions about our world can be asked, and data about those questions can be collected, organized, and analyzed.
- Measurement is approximate. Objects can be measured by making direct comparisons.

Social Emphasis

Socially, experiences in this unit help students to

- Develop appropriate group skills.
- Analyze the effect of behavior on others and on the group work.
- Relate the values of fairness, caring, and responsibility to behavior.

Lessons

This unit includes ten lessons, plus a continuing bulletin board activity. The calendar icon indicates some preparation is needed prior to that lesson.

1. Fraction Puzzles
(page 75)

Team-building lesson for groups of four that helps students understand nonverbal communication.

2. Advertisements
(page 81)

Estimation lesson in which groups estimate the fractional part of a region.

3. Fraction Kits
(page 85)

Fraction kit lesson in which each student makes a fraction kit.

4. Fractions, Fractions!
(page 91)

Fraction lesson in which pairs compare, order, and identify equivalent fractions.

5. Spin It
(page 97)

Spinner activity in which pairs identify equivalent fractions and compare fractions.

6. Say It with Fractions
(page 105)

Fraction kit lesson in which pairs compare, add, and find equivalent fractions.

7. Pencil Investigations 1
(page 111)

Measurement lesson in which groups measure pencils, graph, and discuss the data.

8. Pencil Investigations 2
(page 117)

Data analysis lesson in which groups organize and discuss data.

9. Pencil Investigations 3
(page 121)

Data analysis lesson in which pairs write statements summarizing data.

10. What Do You Think?
(page 125)

Transition lesson in which groups reflect on their work together and write story problems using fractions.

"Fraction of the Week" Bulletin Board

This ongoing activity uses the fraction kit and is to be introduced after Lesson 3. At the beginning of the week, post a fraction on the bulletin board. (The first fraction of the week might be 3/8.) Ask pairs to write at least three factual statements about 3/8, such as "3/8 is larger than 1/4" or "3/8 is one-eighth less than 1/2." Have pairs choose one of their statements, write it in large letters on a sentence strip, and post the statement on the bulletin board. At the end of the week, ask students to use their fraction kits to verify the statements. Ask questions, such as:

Q. Do you agree or disagree with this statement? Why?

Q. How could you rewrite this statement to make it true?

Materials

Throughout the unit, students need access to supplies, such as scissors, pencils, markers, crayons, rulers, and glue sticks. If possible, each group should have a container with these supplies.

The materials needed for the unit are listed below. The first page of each lesson lists the materials specific to that lesson. All blackline masters for transparencies and group record sheets are included at the end of each lesson. Many of the materials are available in the *Number Power* Grade 4 Package.

Teacher Materials

- Bulletin board space for "Fraction of the Week" activity
- Overhead projector, transparency, markers, and chart paper or large newsprint
- Extra "Fraction Puzzles" rectangles (Lesson 1 "Extensions")
- At least four sheets of 8½" × 11" paper per group (Lesson 1 "Extensions")
- 4 envelopes per group (Lesson 1 "Extensions")
- One ½-page advertisement for demonstration (Lesson 2)
- Extra advertisements (Lesson 2 "Extensions")
- A circle, square, and rectangle each cut from different-colored paper (Lesson 3; blackline master included)
- Transparencies of "Fractions, Fractions!" group record sheet (Lesson 4)
- Chart (Lesson 4 "Extensions")
- Extra circles, squares, and rectangles to add to fraction kits (Lessons 3, 4, and 5; blackline master included)
- "Fraction Kits: Extensions" group record sheets (Lesson 3 "Extensions")
- Two spinners for the overhead projector (Lesson 5; blackline master and instructions included)
- "Spin It: Extensions" group record sheets (Lesson 5 "Extensions")
- "Say It with Fractions: Extensions" group record sheets (Lesson 6 "Extensions")
- Transparency of the ruler blackline master (Lesson 7)
- *How Big Is a Foot?* (Lesson 7; optional)
- Interval graph (Lesson 8)
- 3 written statements (Lesson 9)
- Transparency of "Do These Fraction Stories Make Sense?" group record sheet (Lesson 10)

Student Materials

Each student needs

- At least 5 circles, or 5 rectangles, or 5 squares in different colors (Lesson 3; blackline master included)
- Clasp envelope (Lesson 3)

Each pair needs

- One 9" × 12" envelope containing magazine advertisements (Lesson 2)
- "Fractions, Fractions!" group record sheet (Lesson 4)
- Counters (Lessons 4 and 6; optional)
- 2 spinners (Lesson 5; blackline master and instructions included)
- "Do These Fraction Stories Make Sense?" group record sheet (Lesson 10)

Each group of four needs

- 4 envelopes containing puzzle pieces (Lesson 1; blackline master and instructions included)

Teaching Hints

- Prior to each lesson, think about open-ended questions you might ask to extend and probe the thinking of your students. Decide which "Extensions" to have ready when pairs or groups finish early.

- After each lesson, review any "Extensions" students have not explored and decide whether to have students investigate these "Extensions" before going on to the next lesson.

- Encourage students to verbalize their thinking and to write about their thinking when appropriate.

Assessment Techniques

The purpose of the informal assessment questions suggested below is to help you determine your students' understanding of part-to-whole, whole-to-part, and equivalency relationships, as well as their understanding of the relative magnitude of fractions. Students' understanding will vary from experience to experience, particularly as they are beginning to construct their understanding. The assessment techniques suggested here and in the lessons can help you determine what the students seem to understand and can help you make decisions about further experiences students need.

Use the following informal techniques throughout the unit to assess students' understanding of fraction concepts. As you observe, note students' behavior, as well as their conceptual understanding. (For example, some students may give up easily or exhibit a lack of confidence.) Prepare possible questions ahead of time. Accept students' responses without a judgmental reaction, but also probe their thinking by asking follow-up questions that require them to explain further.

Observe Individual Students Working with Fractions

As students work, observe individuals and ask yourself the questions below.

Q. Does the student use fractional notation correctly? Can the student explain the notation?

Note: Students often need many concrete experiences in finding fractional parts of a whole and then connecting that language to the notation before they use the notation correctly. When describing the part-to-whole relationship, stress language such as *[2] out of [6] equal parts*.

Q. Can the student determine the whole when given a part of the whole?

Note: If a student who has been given a part cannot determine the whole, then he or she may need more experiences finding the number of equal parts that make a whole and relating those parts to the whole.

Q. Can the student describe simple equivalency relationships?

Note: Equivalency relationships are often very complex, and require the student to think about several concepts simultaneously. For example, when thinking about the relationships between ½ and ²⁄₄, the student must conceptualize ½ and simultaneously compare ½ to ²⁄₄, noting that both are part of a whole and equivalent to each other. An understanding of these relationships is constructed by the student over time.

Q. Can the student compare and order fractions?

Note: If the student cannot compare and order fractions, he or she may need more experiences comparing fractions with concrete materials and verbalizing why one fraction is larger or smaller than another.

Student Writing

Throughout the unit, ask students to verbalize their thinking, and, at times, to explain their thinking in writing. During this unit, students write

- About their solution to a problem.
- Statements summarizing data.
- About their thinking.
- Story problems using fractions.

UNIT 2 Fractions: Parts and Wholes

Lesson 1

Fraction Puzzles

Students use nonverbal communication to complete four puzzles without talking, then discuss whether each of the four puzzles is divided into equal parts.

Team Builder Emphasis

In this lesson, students

- Begin to develop an effective working relationship.
- Identify equal parts of a whole.
- Add to their understanding that equal parts of a whole are not necessarily congruent.

Social Emphasis

In this lesson, students

- Help each other.
- Communicate nonverbally.

Students continue to

- Develop appropriate group skills.

Group Size: 4

Teacher Materials

- Extra blank fraction puzzle rectangles for "Extensions" (see blackline master)
- At least 4 sheets of 8½" × 11" paper per group for "Extensions"
- 4 envelopes per group for "Extensions"
- Scissors for "Extensions"

Student Materials

Each group of four needs

- 4 envelopes, each containing one piece of each of the 4 puzzles (see "Before the Lesson")

Lesson 1   Fraction Puzzles

75

Before the Lesson

- Before beginning this unit, ask students to write about fractions and about how they have used fractions in their lives. Compare students' current thinking to what they wrote about fractions in Unit 1. Ask yourself questions, such as:

  Q. How has students' thinking changed?

  Q. What further experiences might students need to help them develop their understanding of fractions?

- For each group, make the fraction puzzles by duplicating the blackline master of the four rectangles and cutting the rectangles as indicated. Put one piece from each rectangle into each student's envelope.

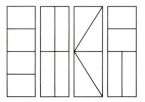

Notes

Teacher

Randomly assign students to groups of four. Explain that the groups will work together throughout the unit.

Introduce the lesson by asking students how they would communicate if they could not talk. List group responses on the chalkboard or on a chart under the heading, "Ways to Communicate Without Talking."

Show the puzzle pieces in one envelope, and state that each group's goal is to make four rectangles of the same size, using all their pieces. Explain that the pieces needed to make the rectangles may be different shapes. Discuss the rules:

1. You may not talk.

2. You may give pieces to others in your group.

3. You may not take pieces from someone else unless they are given to you.

Students

:: ::

:: ::

76   Unit 2   Fractions: Parts and Wholes

Notes	Teacher	Students
Social Emphasis Develop appropriate group skills.	Facilitate a discussion about cooperative behaviors that might help groups work well. Ask questions, such as: Q. Without speaking, how can you let someone know you would like a puzzle piece? Q. Why do you think it is important to make eye contact when you communicate without talking? Hand out the envelopes.	∷ ∷ ∷ ∷
Even if a group has three members, give them the four envelopes and have them make all four rectangles.		
	Observe groups and note how they communicate without talking.	∷ In groups, students complete the puzzles without talking.
Social Emphasis Develop appropriate group skills. **Y**ou might wish to share your observations of the ways students communicated.	Discuss questions as a class, such as: Q. How did you communicate? Q. What ways of communicating seemed to be most helpful? Q. How did someone in your group help you? Q. How would it be different if you could talk?	∷ ∷ ∷ ∷

Lesson 1   Fraction Puzzles

Notes	Teacher	Students
Mathematical Emphasis Equal parts of a whole are not necessarily congruent. Parts are equal when they have the same area. A cooperative structure such as "Heads Together" (see p. xi) can provide opportunities for all students to be involved in the discussion.	Ask groups to look carefully at the pieces that make up each of their four rectangles. First in groups, and then as a class, discuss questions, such as: Q. What do you notice about the puzzle pieces? Q. How can you prove the parts are equal? Q. What are four equal parts of a whole called? [Fourths] Help students reflect on their work together by asking questions, such as: Q. What have you learned about nonverbal communication? How can nonverbal communication be helpful when working with others? Q. What do you want to remember that may help you work together in this unit? Have each group decide on a group name and then share their name with the class.	

Extensions

For Groups That Finish Early

- Give students blank rectangles and ask them to find as many ways as possible to cut a rectangle into four equal parts that are different from the fraction puzzles.

For the Next Day

- Ask groups to make fraction puzzles to share with other groups. Give each group four 8½″ × 11″ sheets of paper. Ask groups to decide how to divide the four sheets of paper so that each sheet is divided into four equal parts that are different from those used in the "Fraction Puzzles" lesson. Ask groups to cut out their puzzle pieces, put one piece from each sheet into each envelope, and trade envelopes with another group.

78 Unit 2 Fractions: Parts and Wholes

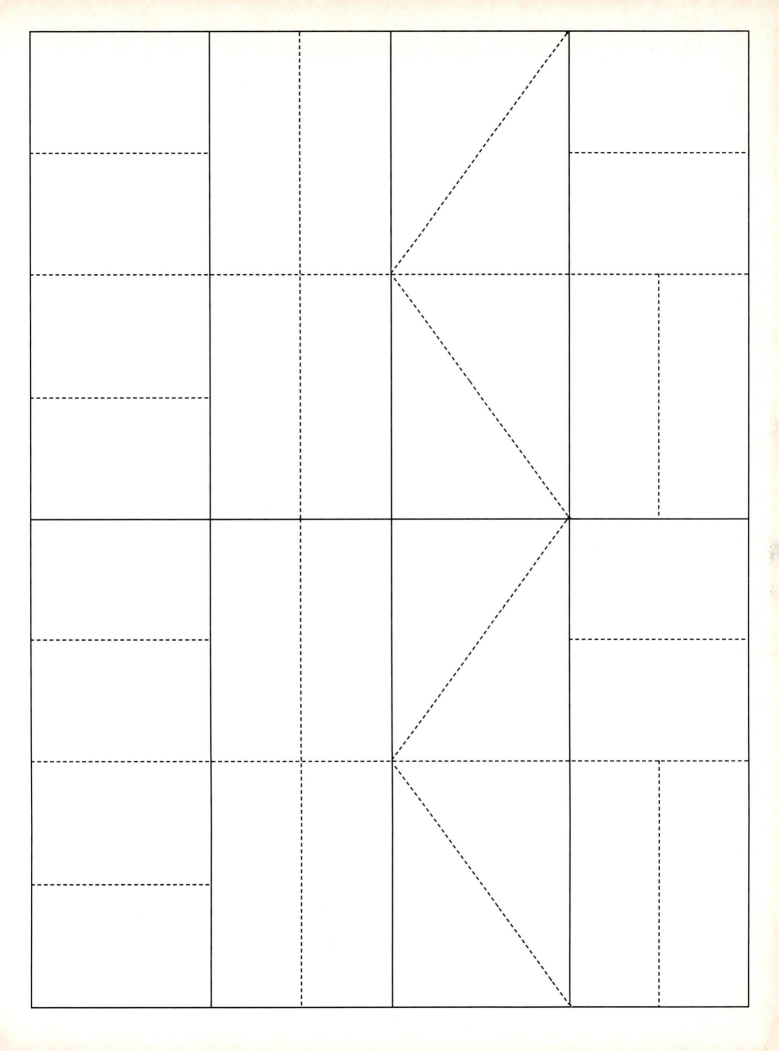

UNIT 2 Fractions: Parts and Wholes

Lesson 2

Advertisements

Students informally estimate the fractional part of a page covered by a magazine advertisement.

Mathematical Emphasis

In this lesson, students

- Estimate.
- Compare parts to the whole.

Students add to their understanding that

- Numbers can be used to describe quantities.
- A unit or set can be subdivided into equal parts.
- Making a reasonable estimate requires gathering and using information.

Social Emphasis

In this lesson, students

- Share the work in a fair way.
- Explain their thinking.

Students continue to

- Develop appropriate group skills.
- Relate the values of fairness, caring, and responsibility to behavior.

Group Size: 2

Teacher Materials

- ½-page advertisement for demonstration (see "Before the Lesson")
- Advertisements for "Extensions" (see "Before the Lesson")

Student Materials

Each pair needs

- 9" × 12" envelope containing magazine advertisements (see "Before the Lesson")
- Pencil and paper
- Scissors

Before the Lesson

- Assemble envelopes containing copies of seven magazine pages for each pair, including pages with ads that cover

  a whole page,
  about ½ of the page horizontally,
  about ½ of the page vertically,
  about ⅓ of the page,
  about ⅔ of the page,
  about ⅙ of the page, and
  about ⅑ of the page.

  If more than one ad is on a page, identify the ad to be used. In each envelope, also include a plain sheet of paper the size of the full magazine page.

- Choose a ½-page ad for introducing and demonstrating the lesson.

- For "Extensions," select three or four ads that are displayed in such a way that it is difficult to tell whether the ad covers more or less than ½ of the page. (For example, an ad might be positioned in the middle of the page, surrounded by text.)

Notes	Teacher	Students

Teacher

Divide groups into pairs. Introduce the lesson and say:

> I was reading a magazine last night and it seemed to me that there were more advertisements than articles. This got me thinking about how much of a page advertisements take in a magazine.

As a class discuss questions, such as:

Q. Why do you think magazines have advertisements?

Q. Why do some advertisers have a small ad and others have an ad that takes the whole page?

Explain that pairs will examine some ads and determine the approximate fractional part of the page the ad covers. Show the ½-page ad and ask pairs to estimate how much of the page the ad covers. Discuss questions, such as:

Q. How much of the page do you think the ad covers?

Q. How could we try to find out? What is another way?

Students

•• ••

•• ••

Notes

Magazines and newspapers sell space by the column inch or by fractional parts of the page.

Discuss the meaning of the word *approximate*.

Model student suggestions for finding the size of the ad. Students might suggest folding the paper to show how many equal parts there are or cutting out the ad and placing it on top of the remaining part of the page to compare.

Unit 2 Fractions: Parts and Wholes

Notes	Teacher	Students
	Show students the contents of one of the envelopes. Explain that pairs will estimate and record the fractional part of the page covered by each ad. First in pairs, and then as a class, have students discuss how they might share the work and how explaining their thinking might help their pairs.	•• •• •• ••
Mathematical Emphasis Making a reasonable estimate requires gathering and using information. As you observe pairs, ask yourself questions, such as: Q. What reasoning did students use to make their estimates? Q. Are students using appropriate fractional notation and language to name the parts? Q. How do you know that students understand such concepts as the number of equal parts that make the whole and that equal parts have the same area?	Observe pairs and, when appropriate, ask questions, such as: Q. Why do you think your estimate is reasonable? What have you done to help you estimate? Q. How are you and your partner sharing the work in a fair way?	•• In pairs, students estimate and record the fractional part of the page covered by each ad.
	First in pairs, then as a class, discuss questions, such as: Q. What did you find out about the approximate sizes of the advertisements? Q. Which ad is the smallest? How do you know? What fraction describes the ad's approximate size? Q. Which ad is the largest? How do you know? What fraction describes the ad's approximate size?	•• •• •• ••

Lesson 2   Advertisements

Notes	Teacher	Students
	Q. Which ads are greater than ½ of the page? How do you know?	•• ••
	Q. Which ads are less than ¼ of the page? How do you know?	•• ••
Social Emphasis Develop appropriate group skills.	Q. How did you and your partner share the work? How did that help?	
	Q. How did you communicate with each other? What methods of nonverbal communication did you use?	
	To help students develop their understanding of fractional relationships, have pairs investigate the activities listed in "Extensions" before going on to the next lesson.	

Extensions

For Pairs That Finish Early

- Ask pairs to discuss the following: One magazine charges about $55,000 to run a full-page ad. About how much would it cost for a ½-page, a ¼-page, and a ¾-page ad? Discuss and write about how you decided the cost of each ad.

- Have students find ads in magazines or newspapers and estimate the fractional part of the page the ad covers.

For the Next Day

- Give pairs the ads that you prepared for the "Extensions" activity (see "Before the Lesson"). Ask pairs to determine whether each ad covers more or less than ½ of a page and to explain or write about their thinking.

- Have 10 students come to the front of the room. Ask 4 of the 10 students to turn their backs to the class. Discuss questions, such as:

  Q. Are more or less than ½ of the students facing the class? How do you know?

  Q. About what fraction of the students are not facing the class? How do you know?

  Have all 10 students face the class again. Choose a different number of students to turn their backs to the class. Ask questions that encourage students to estimate fractional parts of a set.

UNIT 2 Fractions: Parts and Wholes

Lesson 3

Fraction Kits

Students use rectangles, circles, or squares to make a fraction kit. This lesson may take two class periods.

Mathematical Emphasis

In this lesson, students

- Divide regions into fractional parts.

Students add to their understanding that

- A unit or set can be subdivided into equal parts.
- Relationships and equivalencies between quantities can be described.
- Numbers can be used to describe quantities.

Social Emphasis

In this lesson, students

- Help each other.
- Disagree in a kind way.

Students continue to

- Develop appropriate group skills.
- Relate the values of fairness, caring, and responsibility to behavior.

Group Size: 4

Teacher Materials

- A circle, rectangle, and square (see "Before the Lesson")
- Extra circles, squares, and rectangles for adding to fraction kits (see "Before the Lesson")
- "Fraction Kits: Extensions" group record sheets for "Extensions"

Student Materials

Each student will need

- At least 5 shapes in 5 different colors (see "Before the Lesson")
- Scissors
- Clasp envelope (for storing the fraction kit)

Lesson 3   Fraction Kits

85

Before the Lesson

- The students in any one group will make their fraction kits using the same shape. However, in order for students to see a variety of fraction models, one-third of the groups will use circles, one-third will use rectangles, and one-third will use squares. (You may want to make larger rectangles if your students have difficulty manipulating the rectangle on the blackline master.) For this lesson, each student will need at least five of their shape in different colors and extras for experimenting. For "Extensions," students will need two other colors of their shape and extras for experimenting. For the unit, each student will need a different color for each set of fractional parts they make (halves, thirds, fourths, fifths, sixths, eighths, etc.) plus a different color for the shape that represents the whole.

Notes

Model how to fold and then cut the fraction kit if students have not experienced similar activities.

Students may need extra circles, rectangles, or squares as they experiment with folding and cutting the regions into equal parts of the whole.

Social Emphasis
Relate the values of fairness, caring, and responsibility to behavior.

Teacher

Briefly introduce the lesson by explaining that each student will make a fraction kit to use during the unit. Show the circle, rectangle, and square and state that each group will use one of the shapes for their kits. Explain that each student will make a kit that includes a whole shape and shapes that have been cut into halves, fourths, eighths, and sixteenths.

Distribute the materials, making sure all students in a group have the same shape. Ask groups to assign one color to remain as a whole, one to be cut into halves, one to be cut into fourths, etc.

Explain that each student is to fold and cut their four shapes into the fractional parts. Stress the importance of being accurate. Ask students to write their name and the appropriate fractional notation on each piece. Encourage students to help each other and to check each other's kits for accuracy. Ask questions, such as:

Q. How might you check each other's kit?

Q. What are some ways to suggest to someone that a piece needs to be more accurate? How is that a kind way to give this information?

Students

:: ::
:: ::

Unit 2 Fractions: Parts and Wholes

Notes	Teacher	Students

Mathematical Emphasis

A unit or set can be subdivided into equal parts.

As you ask these questions, assess students' understanding of

- how to determine the number of equal parts that make a whole.
- how to divide a region into equal parts.
- how to use fractional notation to name equal parts.

As groups work, ask questions, such as:

Q. How many equal parts make the whole?

Q. How do you know the parts are equal?

Q. How are you helping each other?

Q. Why do you think it is important to check the kits for accuracy?

In groups, students

1. Choose one color to remain as the whole and one color for each of the four fractional parts.

2. Individually cut the four shapes into halves, fourths, eighths, and sixteenths, respectively.

3. Write their names and the appropriate fractional notation on each piece.

4. Check each other's kits for accuracy.

Mathematical Emphasis

Relationships and equivalencies between quantities can be described.

Throughout the unit stress terminology, such as *equal parts of the whole*, *[3] out of [4] equal parts*, and *equivalent to*.

Social Emphasis

Relate the values of fairness, caring, and responsibility to behavior.

First in groups, then as a class, discuss questions, such as:

Q. How many fourths equal a whole? How many sixteenths equal a whole?

Q. How many ways can you make ½? How many ways can you make ¾?

Q. What fractions are larger than ½, but smaller than 1?

Q. What fractions are larger than 0, but smaller than ½?

Have students count by fourths using their fraction kits. For example, as students put ¼ on the whole, they say "one-fourth." As they put another ¼ on the whole, they say "two-fourths," and so on. Ask:

Q. How do you count by eighths? Sixteenths?

Q. How did you act in a caring and responsible way?

Q. How did you communicate with each other? What worked? What didn't work?

Lesson 3 Fraction Kits

Notes	Teacher	Students
	Q. How did your group make sure everyone's kit is accurate? Did anyone have hurt feelings in the group? How did you handle that?	:: :: :: ::
	Q. How did you help each other? Did that help your group? If so, how?	
	To expand students' fraction kits and to help students develop their understanding of fractions, have them investigate the activities in "Extensions" before going on to the next lesson.	

Extensions

For Groups That Finish Early

- Give students shapes in new colors and have them make thirds and sixths for their fraction kits. (Note: Students dividing circles may need many extra circles to experiment with as they make thirds and sixths.) Have students explain to the class how they determined equal parts of the whole.

For the Next Day

- Have pairs discuss the problems on the "Fraction Kits: Extensions" group record sheet. Encourage students to use words such as *about*, *nearly*, and *close to* as they discuss the questions and explain their thinking. (Note: *close to* could be more or less than the amount.)

- Begin "Fraction of the Week," the suggested ongoing activity described in the Overview, p. 70.

Names
_____

Fraction Kits
Extensions

Each of these jars is filled to a different level with pennies. Discuss the questions about the shaded areas of the jars and write about your thinking.

1. Which jars are more than ½ full?

   A

2. Which jars are less than ½ full?

   B

3. About how full is each jar?

   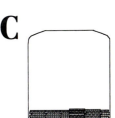

4. Which jars could you combine to fill a new jar so that it is close to ½ full?

5. Which jars could you combine to fill a new jar so that it is nearly full?

   E

6. Which jars could you combine to fill two new jars so they are both nearly full?

   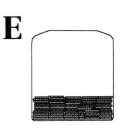

© Addison-Wesley Publishing Company, Inc. Unit 2, Lesson 3: Fraction Kits Group Record Sheet

UNIT 2 Fractions: Parts and Wholes

Lesson 4

Fractions, Fractions!

Students compare and order fractions and identify equivalent fractions. This lesson may take two class periods.

Mathematical Emphasis

In this lesson, students

- Compare and order fractions.
- Identify equivalent fractions.

Students add to their understanding that

- Numbers can be used to describe quantities.
- Relationships and equivalencies between quantities can be described.
- A unit or set can be subdivided into equal parts.

Social Emphasis

In this lesson, students

- Explain their thinking.
- Listen to others.
- Disagree in a kind way.

Students continue to

- Develop appropriate group skills.
- Analyze the effect of behavior on others and on the group work.
- Relate the values of fairness, caring, and responsibility to behavior.

Group Size: 2, and then 4

Teacher Materials

- Extra circles, squares, and rectangles in new colors for adding to fraction kits
- Transparency of the "Fractions, Fractions!" group record sheet
- Chart for "Extensions"

Student Materials

Each pair needs

- Fraction kit (see Lesson 3)
- Pencil and paper
- "Fractions, Fractions!" group record sheet
- Counters (optional)

Lesson 4   Fractions, Fractions!

Notes	Teacher	Students
If students have not already made thirds and sixths, they will need to add these to their fraction kits.	**Divide groups into pairs.** Ask pairs to use the fraction kit they made in "Fraction Kits" (Lesson 3) to explore questions, such as: Q. Show ²/₃. How do you know that it is ²/₃? Q. Show ³/₄. How might you convince a pair with a different shape that you are showing ³/₄?	•• •• •• ••
A cooperative structure, such as "Think, Pair, Share" (see p. xi) can provide opportunities for all students to be involved in the discussion.	Briefly introduce the lesson and explain that pairs will use their fraction kits to solve several fraction problems. Ask pairs to discuss the following problem: **Kiyo and Jesse divided a banana so that Kiyo got ½ and Jesse got ²/₄. Who got more? How do you know?** Have pairs share their thinking and discuss questions, such as: Q. How did you and your partner solve the problem? Q. Was there any disagreement? What did you do?	
Mathematical Emphasis Relationships and equivalencies between quantities can be described.	Q. What do you notice about the two amounts? Q. These fractions are called *equivalent*. What do you think that means? Have pairs use the fraction kit and discuss questions, such as: Q. What is another fraction that is equivalent to ½? How do you know? Q. What fractions are equivalent to ¼? ²/₄? ³/₄? ²/₃? How do you know? Q. Would you prefer ²/₄ of a candy bar or ⁴/₈ of a candy bar? Why?	

Notes	Teacher	Students
	Ask pairs to use their fraction kits and to discuss the following problem:	•• •• •• ••
	Jason has ⅞ of a 10″ pizza and George has ¾ of another 10″ pizza. Jason thinks that his share is closer to a whole pizza than George's. Is he right? How do you know?	
	Ask questions, such as:	
	Q. What is one strategy for solving the pizza problem? Are there other strategies?	
Note that the second problem on the "Fractions, Fractions!" group record sheet involves a set instead of a region. Students may need to use counters instead of the fraction kit.	Hand out one "Fractions, Fractions!" group record sheet to each pair. Show the "Fractions, Fractions!" transparency and explain that pairs will solve the problems, record their solutions, and share their thinking with another pair.	
	Facilitate a discussion about what might help pairs work together. Ask questions, such as:	
Social Emphasis Develop appropriate group skills.	Q. What might help you and your partner work well with another pair?	
	Q. What could you say to another pair if you disagree with their thinking?	
	Observe pairs and ask questions, such as:	•• In pairs, students
	Q. How do you know your solution is reasonable?	1. Solve problems on the "Fractions, Fractions!" group record sheet.
	Q. Which problems have more than one solution? How do you know?	2. Record their solutions and write about their thinking.
		3. Share their thinking with another pair.
	Choose some of the problems to discuss as a class. Ask questions, such as:	•• •• •• ••
	Q. How did you solve the problem?	
	Q. Can the problem be solved in another way?	

Lesson 4   Fractions, Fractions!

Notes	Teacher	Students
Social Emphasis Analyze the effect of behavior on others and on the group work.	Help students reflect on their work together. Ask questions, such as: Q. What did you and your partner do when you did not agree to a solution? What happened as a result? Q. What did the pairs in your group do when they did not agree with each other's solution? How do you feel about the way you communicated with each other? What would you do differently or the same next time? To help students develop their understanding of relative magnitude of fractions, have pairs investigate the activities listed in "Extensions" before going on to the next lesson.	•• •• •• ••

Extensions

For Pairs That Finish Early

- Ask pairs to investigate the following and to record their thinking:

  1. Find at least three fractions that are greater than ¼ but less than 1.
  2. Find a fraction that is close to 0.
  3. Find a fraction that is close to ½.
  4. Find a fraction that is close to 1.
  5. Find a fraction between ¼ and ½.
  6. Find numbers that are greater than 2/4 but less than 2.

For the Next Day

- Post charts labeled as follows:

  Fractions that are greater than ¼ but less than 1
  Fractions that are close to 0
  Fractions that are close to ½
  Fractions that are close to 1
  Fractions that are between ¼ and ½
  Numbers that are greater than 1 but less than 2

  Have pairs decide on and then list fractions on each chart. First in pairs, then as a class, ask students to discuss the fractions listed on the charts and to decide whether they think the fractions are correctly categorized. Have students discuss and justify their thinking.

- Continue with the "Fraction of the Week" activity described in the Overview, p. 70.

Names

Fractions, Fractions!

1. Carla was exploring her fraction kit. She decided to find fractions greater than ¾. She found ⅔, ⅝, ⅚, and ½. Do you agree? Explain. What other fractions could you suggest to Carla that are greater than ¾ but less than 1?

2. Laticha promised to give her brother a little less than ½ of her penny collection on his birthday. What fraction of her penny collection could she give him? How do you know? Laticha has 103 pennies. About how many pennies could she give to her brother?

3. Han and Maria were playing a fraction game called Guess My Fraction. Han gave the clue, "I am thinking of a fraction between ½ and ¾." What might Han's fraction be? How do you know? Can you be sure you know his fraction? Explain.

4. Three friends were eating oranges. Roberto ate ⅜ of an orange, Hiroko ate ¼ of an orange, and Michael ate ½ of an orange. Who ate the most? Who ate the least? How do you know? How many whole oranges did they have? How do you know?

5. Kevin and Nick went to the pizza shop. They each ordered a small pepperoni pizza. Kevin asked the pizza maker to cut his pizza into 6 equal slices. Nick asked him to cut his pizza into 8 equal slices. Kevin ate 4 slices of his pizza. Nick ate 5 slices of his pizza. They wondered who had eaten the most pizza. What do you think? How can you prove it?

UNIT 2 Fractions: Parts and Wholes

Lesson 5

Spin It

Students spin two spinners and use the numbers generated to write the smallest possible fraction. Students spin again, write a second fraction, and then compare the two fractions.

Mathematical Emphasis

In this lesson, students

- Compare fractions.
- Identify equivalent fractions.

Students add to their understanding that

- The relative magnitude of numbers can be described.
- Relationships and equivalencies between quantities can be described.
- Numbers can be used to describe quantities.

Social Emphasis

In this lesson, students

- Explain their thinking.
- Check for agreement.

Students continue to

- Develop appropriate group skills.
- Analyze the effect of behavior on others and on the group work.

Group Size: 2

Teacher Materials

- Overhead projector and markers
- 2 spinners for the overhead projector (see "Before the Lesson")
- Extra circles, squares, and rectangles for adding to fraction kits
- "Spin It: Extensions" group record sheets for "Extensions"

Student Materials

Each pair needs

- Fraction kit (see Lesson 3)
- 2 spinners (see "Before the Lesson")
- Pencil and paper

Before the Lesson

- Make spinners using the blackline master (see blackline master for directions).

- Students will need halves, thirds, fourths, sixths, eighths, ninths, and twelfths in their fraction kits for this activity. Have students add whatever fraction pieces they need.

Notes	Teacher	Students
For example, if one spinner lands on 4 and the other spinner on 6, the two possible fractions would be 6/4 and 4/6. For this lesson, do not be concerned with simplifying the fractions. If both spinners land on the same number, ask, "What do we know about a fraction like 4/4 or 8/8?"	Introduce the lesson by spinning two spinners on the overhead projector. Ask pairs to write the smallest possible fraction using the two numbers. Encourage students to use their fraction kits to help them determine the smallest possible fraction. Ask questions, such as: **Q. What fractions could you make by using the two numbers? Which is smaller? How do you know?** Spin the two spinners two more times, each time asking pairs to make the smallest possible fraction. Have pairs discuss and compare the two fractions. Ask questions, such as: **Q. How do the two fractions compare to each other? What relationships do you notice?**	•• •• •• ••
Students may need to be reminded what the term *equivalent* means. Ask: **Q.** What are some examples of equivalent fractions? How do you know they are equivalent?	**Q. Are the fractions equivalent? How do you know?** **Q. Which fraction is larger? How do you know? Is there another way to explain which is larger?** Repeat this activity, then have pairs continue the activity. Explain that they are to 1. Each spin a spinner. 2. Write the smallest possible fraction using the numbers they have generated. 3. Repeat this process. 4. Compare and write about the two resulting fractions.	

Unit 2 Fractions: Parts and Wholes

Notes	Teacher	Students

As you observe pairs, ask yourself:

Q. How do students show they understand how to make the smallest possible fraction?

Q. How do students demonstrate an understanding of equivalency?

Q. How do students show they are able to compare and order fractions?

Observe pairs and ask questions, such as:

Q. What can you say about these two fractions?

Q. How do you know these two fractions are equivalent?

Q. Why is this fraction larger?

Q. How are you checking to be sure you both agree?

•• In pairs, students

1. Use spinners to generate numbers and write the smallest possible fraction.

2. Repeat the process.

3. Compare and write about the two fractions.

4. Continue with the activity.

Mathematical Emphasis

Relationships and equivalencies between quantities can be described.

Social Emphasis

Analyze the effect of behavior on others and on the group work.

Help students reflect on the lesson by asking questions, such as:

Q. What relationships did you write about?

Q. What equivalent fractions did you find? How do you know they are equivalent?

Q. Which of the fractions are equal to a whole? Why?

Q. Which of the fractions are greater than a whole? How do you know?

Q. How did your behavior affect your work?

Q. What things did you do that helped you work as a pair? What things did you do that did not help you work as a pair?

To help students develop their understanding of fractions, have pairs investigate the activities in "Extensions" before going on to the next lesson.

•• ••

•• ••

Lesson 5 Spin It

 **Extensions**

For Pairs That Finish Early

- Ask pairs to spin the two spinners three times, each time making the smallest possible fraction. Have students order the three fractions from smallest to largest. Have students repeat this activity several times.

For the Next Day

- Have pairs solve the problems on the "Spin It: Extensions" group record sheet.

- Continue with the "Fraction of the Week" activity described in the Overview, p. 70.

Names

Directions for Making Spinners

Materials for one spinner

- Spinner face (copy blackline master and cut; copy on a transparency for the overhead spinners)
- 3" × 5" index card
- 3/8" piece of a drinking straw
- paper clip or a bobby pin
- ruler
- tape

Instructions

1. Bend up the outside part of the paper clip as shown (or open up a bobby pin) and use the point to poke a hole in the center of the spinner face.

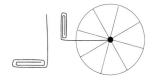

2. Poke a hole in the center of an index card with the paper clip or bobby pin and draw a line from the center to one corner.

3. Cut a piece of masking tape about 2" long.

4. Poke the paper clip or bobby pin through the center of the index card and tape it on the bottom of the card to hold it in place. (The top of the card has the line.)

5. Put the 3/8" piece of drinking straw on the paper clip or bobby pin that is sticking through the top of the card. It will serve as a washer to keep the spinner face off the index card.

6. Put the spinner face on next.

7. Cover the point of the paper clip with a piece of tape to keep the spinner from spinning off (this step can be omitted if using a bobby pin).

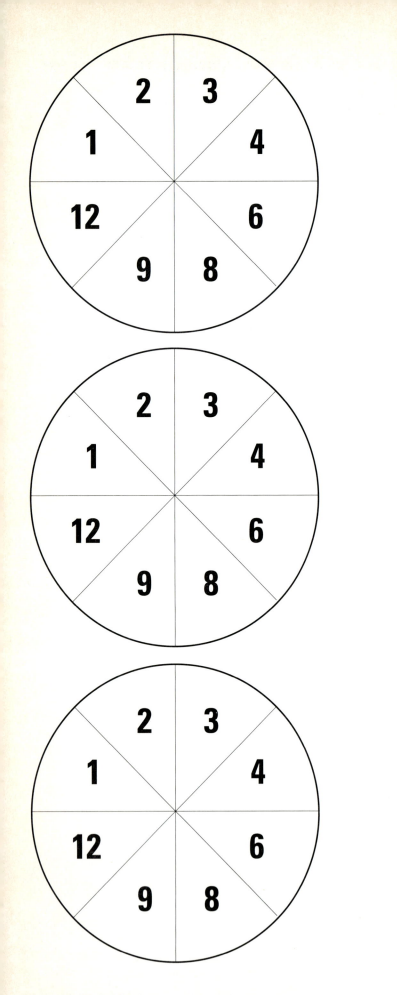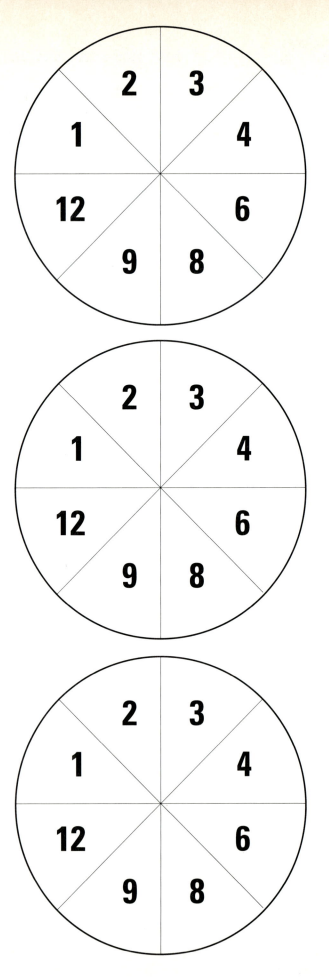

Names

Spin It
Extension

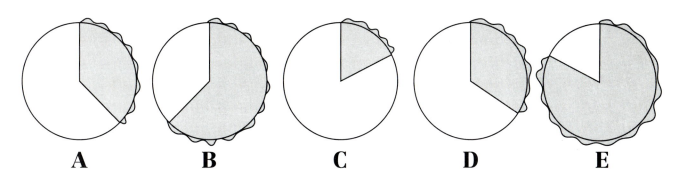

A B C D E

Each of these pies have slices missing. The shaded areas show the pie that is left. Discuss the following questions and write about your thinking.

1. Which pies have more than 1/3 left?

2. Which pies have less than 1/3 left?

3. About what fractional part of each pie is left?

4. Which pies could you combine to make a pie that is almost whole?

5. Which pies could you combine to make two almost complete pies?

6. Put 3 of the pies together. About how much pie do you have?

UNIT 2 FRACTIONS: Parts and Wholes

Lesson 6

Say It with Fractions

Students compare and order fractions and write fraction statements. This lesson may take two class periods.

Mathematical Emphasis

In this lesson, students

- Compare and order fractions.
- Identify equivalent fractions.
- Write fraction statements.

Students add to their understanding that

- Numbers can be used to describe quantities.
- Relationships and equivalencies between quantities can be described.
- A unit or set can be subdivided into equal parts.

Social Emphasis

In this lesson, students

- Share the work in a fair way.
- Disagree in a kind way.

Students continue to

- Develop appropriate group skills.
- Analyze the effect of behavior on others and on the group work.

Group Size: 2, and then 4

Teacher Materials

- "Say It with Fractions: Extensions" group record sheets for "Extensions"

Student Materials

Each pair needs

- Fraction kit (see Lesson 3)
- Counters (optional)
- Pencil and paper

Lesson 6 Say It with Fractions

105

Notes	Teacher	Students
A cooperative structure such as "Turn To Your Partner" (see p. xi) provides opportunities for all students to be involved in the discussion.	Introduce the lesson by stating that pairs will use their understanding of fractions to determine whether some mathematical statements are true or false. Ask students to help you count the number of people in the room. Record this number on the chalkboard. Ask anyone wearing clothing with visible words or letters to stand. As a class, count the number of people standing. Record this number on the chalkboard. First in pairs, then as a class, discuss questions, such as:	•• •• •• ••

Q. Is more or less than ½ the class standing? How do you know?

Q. About what fraction of the whole class is standing? How close is that to the whole class? How do you know?

Write at least three of the following statements (or similar statements) on the chalkboard.

1. ³⁄₆ of the set of marbles is not equal to ½ of the set of marbles.

2. ½ of a yard of fabric is greater than ⅛ of a yard and ²⁄₄ of a yard together.

3. ⅝ of an cake minus ⅛ of a cake equals ½ of a cake.

4. ¼ of the class plus ⅛ of the class plus ½ of the class equals the whole class.

5. ⅜ of an inch is closer to zero than to ½ of an inch.

As a class, discuss the first statement.

Q. How can you prove that this statement is true or false? Is there another way to explain it?

Model how students might write about their thinking, for example: "We know that ⅝ minus ⅛ is the same as ⁴⁄₈, and ⁴⁄₈ is equivalent to ½, so the statement is true."

Write students' explanations on the chalkboard.

Unit 2 Fractions: Parts and Wholes

Notes	Teacher	Students
Students may choose to use their fraction kits or counters to help them solve the problems.	**A**sk pairs to discuss the remaining statements and decide whether the statements are true or false. Ask pairs to record their explanation for one of the statements.	•• In pairs, students 1. Discuss each statement and decide whether it is true or false. 2. Write about their thinking for one statement.
	Have a few pairs share their written explanations, and ask questions, such as: Q. **What questions would you like to ask this pair to help you understand their explanation?** Q. **What did you learn by listening to other pairs' explanations?**	•• •• •• ••
Leave the statements from the first part of this lesson posted as examples. Help students recognize that the statements have different purposes. Some compare fractions, others show addition or subtraction of fractions, and some discuss equivalence. **Social Emphasis** Analyze the effect of behavior on others and on the group work.	Explain that pairs are to write at least three true or false statements about fractions—statements that compare, order, add, subtract, or show equivalence—and exchange the statements with another pair. Pairs are to use fraction kits to verify the other pair's statements, then discuss all six statements with the other pair. Ask questions, such as: Q. **Think about a time when someone disagreed with you. What happened? How did it make you feel?** Q. **Think about a time when you disagreed with someone. What happened? How did the other person feel?** Q. **What are some things to remember if you and your partner disagree with the other pair or do not understand their explanation?**	

Lesson 6 Say It with Fractions

Notes	Teacher	Students

As you observe, assess pairs' statements. Ask yourself questions, such as:

Q. Do students write a variety of statements? Are they, for example, writing only comparative statements such as "½ of a pizza is greater than ¼ of a pizza" and "⅓ is smaller than ½"?

Q. Do students understand the statement? How do they explain their thinking? Are their explanations logical? What do their explanations show about their understanding of fractions?

Observe pairs and, when appropriate, ask questions, such as:

Q. How do you know your statement is true?

Q. How do your statements differ from each other?

Q. Did you write any false statements? Why are they false?

•• In pairs, students

1. Write three true or false statements comparing, ordering, adding, or subtracting fractions.

2. Exchange statements with another pair and verify the statements.

3. Share their thinking about the six statements with the other pair.

Social Emphasis
Analyze the effect of behavior on others and on the group work.

Help students reflect on the lesson by asking questions, such as:

Q. Which statements were the most challenging to verify? Why?

Q. How did you disagree? What effect did that disagreement have on your work?

Q. How did you and your partner share the work? How did each partner contribute? How did that help your pair work?

•• ••

•• ••

Extensions

For Pairs That Finish Early

- Have pairs exchange written statements with different pairs in the class and verify the statements.

For the Next Day

- Have pairs solve the problems on the "Say It with Fractions: Extensions" group record sheets.

108   Unit 2   Fractions: Parts and Wholes

Names

Say It with Fractions
Extensions

Imagine that you sell ads for the school newspaper, *The School Times*. Discuss the ad rate chart and the problems. Write about your thinking.

The School Times Ad Rates

Full page	$20.00	⅓ page	$9.00
3/4 page	$18.00	1/4 page	$7.75
⅔ page	$15.50	⅙ page	$6.00
½ page	$12.75	⅛ page	$3.50

1. The sports page has stories that will cover three-fourths of the page. Mr. Yu would like to place a ⅛-page ad on that page. Is there enough room? How do you know? Is there room for any other ads? If so, what size? How do you know?

2. One page of the paper is only for advertisements. The ad department decided to put three advertisements on this page and charge a total of $27.50 for these ads. What size ads are on the page? How can you show that the ads total one whole page?

3. One-half of the entertainment page has stories. What combinations of ads would fit on the rest of the page?

4. One-half of the school activities page has stories. The Pizza Shop wants a ⅔-page ad on that page. Is that possible?

5. The safety page already has three ⅙-page ads. How much space is left for stories? How do you know? How much do the three ads cost?

6. One page of the paper has stories that fill one-half of the page and an ad that fills one-fourth of the page. How much of the page is left? How do you know? What combination of ads might fit in that space?

UNIT 2 Fractions: Parts and Wholes

Lesson 7

Pencil Investigations 1

Students measure pencils, graph their results on a number line, and discuss the data.

Mathematical Emphasis

In this lesson, students

- Measure with a ruler.
- Graph results.
- Summarize information.

Students add to their understanding that

- Measurement is approximate. Objects can be measured by making direct comparisons.
- Relationships and equivalencies between quantities can be described.
- Questions about our world can be asked, and data about those questions can be collected, organized, and analyzed.

Social Emphasis

In this lesson, students

- Share the work in a fair way.
- Help each other.

Students continue to

- Develop appropriate group skills.
- Analyze the effect of behavior on others and on the group work.

Group Size: 4

Teacher Materials

- Overhead projector
- Transparency of the ruler blackline master
- *How Big Is a Foot?* (optional; see "Before the Lesson")

Student Materials

Each group needs

- At least 8 pencils of different lengths
- Pencil and paper
- Inch ruler marked to at least a fourth of an inch (can be made using the ruler blackline master)

 **Before the Lesson**

- If students have had little previous experience with standard measurement, provide many opportunities to use and discuss standard units, including fractional parts of those units, and to measure and compare objects.

- If possible, read aloud and discuss the story *How Big Is a Foot?* by Rolf Myller (Atheneum Publishers, 1972). Discuss the need for standard measurement.

Notes

Students will probably suggest measuring all the pencils in the class. If not, decide whether to explore any of the alternative ideas and/or to suggest this strategy.

Students might say that the pencil is about 7½ inches, or almost 7¾ inches, or a little more than 7½ inches, or between 7½ inches and 7¾ inches. Some students might suggest measuring the pencil to the nearest eighth of an inch. If so, have students demonstrate dividing the ruler into eighths.

Teacher

Introduce the lesson by telling the following story:

> The other day I was with a friend and she was using one of the longest pencils I had ever seen. It was a little longer than 13 inches. I started thinking about the typical length of the pencils in our class. What do you think the typical length of our pencils might be?

Discuss questions, such as:

Q. **What does *typical* mean?** [The most frequent length]

Q. **What do you think the typical length of all the pencils in our class might be?**

Q. **How could we find out?**

Show the transparency of a ruler. Place a pencil on the overhead and ask questions, such as:

Q. **How long is this pencil? Is it closer to [7½ inches or 7¾ inches]? How might you write that measurement?**

Q. **Do you think this pencil is typical of the pencils in our class? Why?**

Explain that in order to gather data about this question, groups will measure all their pencils and record their lengths.

Students

∷ ∷

∷ ∷

112 Unit 2 Fractions: Parts and Wholes

Notes	Teacher	Students
	Facilitate a discussion about working as a group. Ask questions, such as: Q. What has helped you work well as a group? Q. What do you think will help you work as a group today?	:: :: :: ::
It makes for a richer discussion if groups have at least 8 pencils.	Ask students to take all the pencils out of their desks or group containers. Collect pencils from anywhere else in the room and distribute them to the groups.	
ASSESSMENT **O**bserve groups and ask yourself the following questions: Q. When measuring objects, do students align the object with the zero on the ruler? Q. Do students use appropriate fractional notation? Can they write mixed numbers? Q. Do students understand equivalency concepts and notations? (For example, ½ can be read as 2/4 or 4/8.)	**O**bserve groups and, when appropriate, ask questions, such as: Q. How are you sharing the work? How are you helping each other? Q. How are you recording the measurements? Q. What fractions are equivalent to ½? ¼? ¾?	:: In groups, students measure and record the lengths of pencils.
	Make a number line on the chalkboard (see example below). Begin numbering at 0, and ask students to suggest, based on the data they have collected, how far to extend it and into what fractional parts to divide the number line. As a class decide how to record eighths on the number line, if some students have measured to the nearest eighth of an inch. 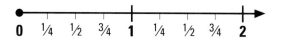 0 ¼ ½ ¾ 1 ¼ ½ ¾ 2	:: :: :: ::
	Have groups copy the number line, and then record their data on it.	:: In groups, students copy a number line from the chalkboard, and record their data on it.

Lesson 7 Pencil Investigations 1

Notes	Teacher	Students

Mathematical Emphasis

Questions about our world can be asked, and data about those questions can be collected, organized, and analyzed.

After groups have marked their number lines, ask questions, such as:

Q. How might you summarize your data?

Q. How many pencils did you measure?

Q. Are more than half of your pencils more than 5 inches? How do you know?

Explain that in the next lesson groups will plot their data on a class graph. Have students predict how that graph might look. Ask questions, such as:

Q. Do you think that more than half of the pencils will be close to 6 inches long or longer? Why?

Q. What do you think the typical pencil length for the class will be?

Social Emphasis

Analyze the effect of behavior on others and on the group work.

Help students reflect on their group work by asking questions, such as:

Q. What behaviors were helpful to the group? How were they helpful?

Q. How did your group share the work? How did that help your work?

Collect each group's list of pencil lengths and number lines for use in the next lesson.

Extensions

For Groups That Finish Early
- Ask groups to write three summary statements about the data on their number line, using fractions when possible. Have groups exchange statements and number lines and decide if the statements are accurate.

For the Next Day
- Continue with the next lesson, "Pencil Investigations 2."

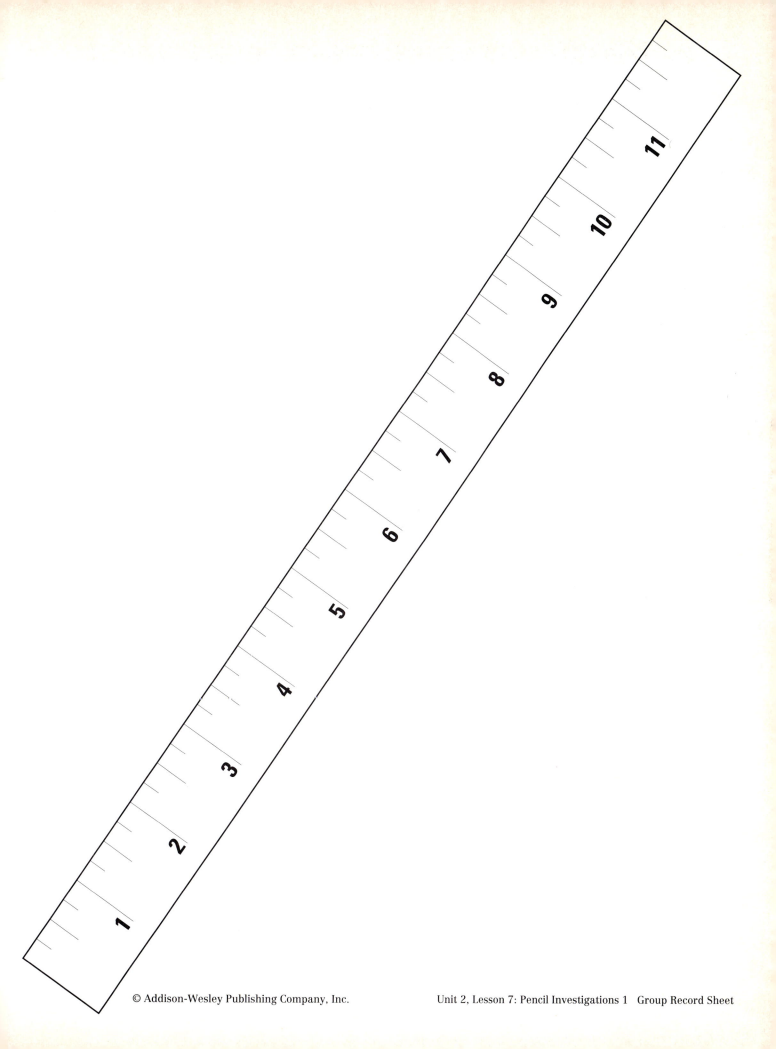

© Addison-Wesley Publishing Company, Inc.   Unit 2, Lesson 7: Pencil Investigations 1   Group Record Sheet

UNIT 2 Fractions: Parts and Wholes

Lesson 8

Pencil Investigations 2

On a class graph, students record the data they collected during "Pencil Investigations 1," then compare and interpret the data.

DAYS AHEAD 1

Teacher Materials
- Interval graph (see "Before the Lesson")
- Marker

Student Materials
Each group needs
- Number line from Lesson 7
- Pencil and paper

Mathematical Emphasis
In this lesson, students
- Graph results.
- Interpret data.

Students add to their understanding that
- Questions about our world can be asked, and data about those questions can be collected, organized, and analyzed.
- Relationships and equivalencies between quantities can be described.
- Numbers can be used to describe quantities.

Social Emphasis
In this lesson, students
- Explain their thinking.
- Listen to others.

Students continue to
- Develop appropriate group skills.
- Analyze the effect of behavior on others and on the group work.

Group Size: 4

Lesson 8 Pencil Investigations 2

Before the Lesson

- Make the following graph on a large piece of paper. This graph will also be used in the next lesson.

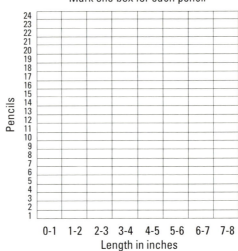

Notes	Teacher	Students
	Ask students to discuss what they discovered in the previous lesson. Explain that students will make a class graph using the information they collected. Display and discuss the blank graph, asking questions, such as:	∷ ∷ ∷ ∷
If the term is new to students, discuss the meaning of *interval*.	**Q. In which interval would a pencil that is about 5 ½ inches long be marked? How do you know?**	
	Q. In which interval would a pencil that is about 4 inches long be marked? What problem do you have making this decision? (The length could be recorded in the interval 3–4 inches or 4–5 inches.)	
To record data in a consistent manner, the class will need to decide whether a 3-inch pencil, for example, should be noted in the third or fourth interval.	As a class, decide where to mark measures that are whole numbers. Ask: **Q. What do you know about the lengths of the pencils that are in the 4–5 inch interval? The 3–4 inch interval?**	

118   Unit 2   Fractions: Parts and Wholes

Notes	Teacher	Students
	Have groups decide the interval in which the lengths of their pencils should be recorded and the number of pencils to record in each interval.	∷ In groups, students review their data and decide where to record it on the graph.
Groups should mark one box for each pencil (i.e., if a group has two 3½-inch pencils, they will mark two boxes in the 3–4 inch interval).	**H**ave groups record on the graph. Discuss the data as the graph changes. After half the groups have marked the graph, ask: Q. Half of the groups put their data on the graph. What do you think the graph will look like when we have all the data? Why?	∷ ∷ ∷ ∷
Typical means usual or, in this case, the interval or intervals where data are clustered. For example, in the graph below, the length of the typical pencil is between 3 and 6 inches. 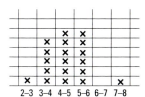However, in the graph below, the data do not indicate a typical length. 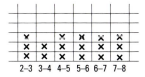The data might reveal more than one typical length, such as in the graph below. 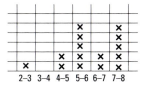	First in pairs, then as a class, discuss the completed graph. Ask questions, such as: Q. What do you notice about the data? Q. What statements can you make about the data? Q. Where are the data clumped? Q. Are there any holes that contain no data? Why do you think that has happened? Are the data spread out? Why do you think that has happened? Q. What is the length of the class' *typical* pencil? Why do you think that? How many pencils are recorded in that interval? About what fractional part of the total number of pencils is that? How do you know? Q. Are more or less than half the pencils longer than [4 inches]? How do you know? Q. About what fraction of the pencils is longer than [5 inches]? Q. How do the data on your number line compare with the data on the graph?	

Notes	Teacher	Students
Social Emphasis Analyze the effect of behavior on others and on the group work.	Help students reflect on their interaction by asking questions, such as: Q. In what ways did group members show they were listening to each other? Q. How did the behavior of your group affect your work? Q. Think to yourself. Did you share your thinking today? In what ways did you help your group? Explain that students will work with these data again in the next lesson.	

Extensions

For Groups That Finish Early

- Ask groups to write five questions that could be answered by analyzing the graph and two questions that could not be answered by analyzing the graph.

For the Next Day

- Continue with the "Fraction of the Week" activity described in the Overview, p. 70.

- Continue with the next lesson, "Pencil Investigations 3."

UNIT 2 Fractions: Parts and Wholes

Lesson 9

Pencil Investigations 3

Students work in pairs and in groups of four to write statements summarizing information on the pencil graph.

Mathematical Emphasis

In this lesson, students

- Write summary statements.
- Interpret data.
- Use fractions.

Students add to their understanding that

- Questions about our world can be asked, and data about those questions can be collected, organized, and analyzed.
- Relationships and equivalencies between quantities can be described.
- Numbers can be used to describe quantities.

Social Emphasis

In this lesson, students

- Listen to others.
- Explain their thinking.

Students continue to

- Develop appropriate group skills.
- Relate the values of fairness, caring, and responsibility to behavior.

Group Sizes: 2, and then 4

Teacher Materials

- 3 statements regarding pencil graph data (see "Before the Lesson")
- Overhead projector (optional)
- Interval graph (see Lesson 8)

Student Materials

Each pair needs

- Pencil and paper
- Pencil graph data (see Lesson 8)

Lesson 9   Pencil Investigations 3

121

Before the Lesson

- On the chalkboard, a chart, or an overhead transparency, write three statements about the data on the class graph from 'Pencil Investigations 2" (Lesson 8). Include at least one false statement. For example:

  About half of the pencils are longer than 5 inches.

  More pencils are in the 3–4 inch interval than in any other interval.

  20 out of the 56 pencils are between 4 and 5 inches long.

Notes	Teacher	Students
	Display the class graph from "Pencil Investigations 2." Explain that students will work in pairs and then in groups to write statements about data. Show the three statements you have written and, as a class, discuss whether the first statement is true or false. Ask pairs to discuss the remaining two statements, to explain their thinking to the other pair in their group, listen to the thinking of the other pair, and to try to come to an agreement about whether the statements are true or false.	•• •• •• ••
	As pairs work, ask questions, such as: Q. How are you showing your partner that you are listening to his or her ideas? Q. How do you know this statement is true [false]? Q. How is the other pair showing that they are listening to your ideas? How does that make you feel? Q. How are you checking to see that you all agree? Q. How has the other pair disagreed with your thinking? How does that make you feel?	•• •• In groups, students 1. Work with a partner to decide if the two statements are true or false. 2. Explain their thinking to the other pair in their group.

122   Unit 2   Fractions: Parts and Wholes

Notes	Teacher	Students
Encourage students to make statements such as "9 out of 50 pencils are between 2 and 3 inches long," as well as to use fractions.	As a class, discuss the statements. Then ask students to help you write one or two true statements about the data, and one or two false statements about the data. Explain that pairs are to write three summary statements about the information on the graph, one of which is false, then exchange their statements with the other pair in their group. Pairs are then to decide if the other pair's statements are true or false, and discuss their thinking with the other pair.	•• •• •• ••
Mathematical Emphasis Questions about our world can be asked, and data about those questions can be collected, organized, and analyzed.	As groups work, ask questions, such as: Q. What is helping you work? Q. Is this statement true or false? How do you know? Q. What statements using fractions can you make about the data? Q. How is the other pair showing they are listening to your ideas? How does that make you feel?	•• In groups, students •• 1. Work with a partner to write three summary statements, including one false statement. 2. Exchange statements with the other pair in their group, and decide whether the pair's statements are true or false. 3. Share their thinking with the other pair.

Lesson 9   Pencil Investigations 3

Notes	Teacher	Students
Social Emphasis Relate the values of fairness, caring, and responsibility to behavior.	Help students reflect on the lesson by asking questions, such as: Q. **Think to yourself. How were you a responsible group member?** Q. **How was your partner a responsible group member?**	:: :: :: ::
If students indicate that they had problems working in pairs or groups, ask questions, such as: Q. What behavior got in the way? Q. What could be done differently next time? As a student describes a behavior that might help the group function better, ask questions, such as: Q. How is that a responsible way to act? Q. How is that fair?	Q. **What behaviors helped your pair or group? What behaviors caused problems for your pair or group?** Collect students' summary statements to use for "Extensions For the Next Day."	

Extensions

For Pairs That Finish Early

- Have pairs write three questions that can be answered using information from the graph and one question that cannot be answered using information from the graph. Collect these questions for use in the "For the Next Day" activity.

For the Next Day

- Hand out students' summary statements to other pairs. Have pairs decide whether the statements are true or false.

- Ask pairs to answer questions written by students in the "For Pairs That Finish Early" activity.

- Continue with the "Fraction of the Week" activity described in the Overview, p. 70.

UNIT 2 Fractions: Parts and Wholes   Lesson 10

What Do You Think?

Students solve fraction story problems, write a fraction story problem for a class fraction book, and reflect on their work together in this unit. This lesson may take two periods.

Transition Emphasis
In this lesson, students
- Reflect on how they worked together and talk about how they might work differently next time.
- Thank each other and say good-bye.
- Write and solve problems.

Social Emphasis
In this lesson, students
- Listen to others.
- Give reasons for opinions.
- Check for understanding.

Students continue to
- Develop appropriate group skills.
- Relate the values of fairness, caring, and responsibility to behavior.

Teacher Materials
- Overhead projector and markers
- Transparency of "Do These Fraction Stories Make Sense?" group record sheet

Student Materials
Each pair needs
- "Do These Fraction Stories Make Sense?" group record sheet

Each group needs
- 2 pieces of paper and a pencil

Group Sizes: 2, and then 4

Lesson 10   What Do You Think?   125

Notes	Teacher	Students
	Help students review their work in this unit by asking questions, such as:	•• •• •• ••

Q. How have you used fractions?

Q. What have you learned about fractions?

Show and read the first story on the "Do These Fraction Stories Make Sense?" transparency:

> Johnny ordered a small pizza. The pizza maker asked if Johnny would like his pizza cut into four slices or eight slices. Johnny thought for a minute and said, "Better make it four slices, I'm not hungry enough to eat eight slices!"

Have pairs discuss whether Johnny's answer makes sense. Ask questions, such as:

Q. What questions might you ask Johnny to find out what he was thinking?

Q. Does Johnny's answer make sense? How do you know?

Explain that students will solve two more fraction stories and write story problems for a class fraction book.

Social Emphasis
Develop appropriate group skills.

As a class, discuss what might help pairs work effectively. Ask questions, such as:

Q. Why do you think it is important to explain your opinion?

Q. How might you make sure your partner understands your thinking? How might you be sure you understand your partner's thinking?

Hand out the "Do These Fraction Stories Make Sense?" group record sheets. Ask pairs to read and discuss the second and third stories and record their thinking.

Notes	Teacher	Students
	Observe pairs and, when appropriate, ask questions, such as: Q. Does the story make sense? How do you know? Q. What are some of your ideas about how to solve the problems?	•• In pairs, students 1. Read and discuss the fraction stories. 2. Decide whether the stories make sense.
Encourage students to ask each other clarifying questions in order to understand others' solutions.	**A**sk several pairs to report their solutions to the fraction stories, encouraging them to explain and clarify their solutions to the class. Ask questions, such as: Q. What strategy did you use to solve the second fraction story? The third? What other strategies might work? Q. How did listening to each other help your work?	•• •• •• ••
	Explain that pairs will work with the other pair in their group and brainstorm possible story problems using fractions. Ask groups to write a story that makes sense on one page, and a story that does not make sense on another page. Ask groups to write their thinking about the story on the back of each page. Ask questions, such as: Q. How does each story on the group record sheet end? [With a question] Q. What do you know about fractions that might help you write story problems using fractions?	:: :: :: ::

Lesson 10   What Do You Think?

Notes	Teacher	Students
A cooperative structure such as "Group Brainstorming" (see p. xi) can provide opportunities for all students to share, analyze, and synthesize their ideas.	Observe groups, and, when appropriate, ask questions, such as: Q. What are some of your ideas for stories? Q. What does a person need to know about fractions to be able to solve this problem?	∙∙ In groups, students 1. Brainstorm possible fraction story problems. 2. Write two fraction story problems, one that makes sense and one that does not. 3. Explain their thinking on the back of each page.
Social Emphasis Relate the values of fairness, caring, and responsibility to behavior. **A** cooperative structure such as "Heads Together" (see p. xi) can provide opportunities for all students to be involved in the discussion.	Have groups share their fraction story problems with the class. First in groups, then as a class, discuss the groups' stories. As a class, reflect on the behaviors that helped groups work fairly and responsibly during this unit. Ask questions, such as: Q. What did you like about the way your group worked together during this unit? What would you do differently next time? Q. What did you do to make decisions when you had different ideas? Q. What did you learn about sharing work fairly? Being responsible for your own behavior? Helping others? Give groups an opportunity to thank each other and to say good-bye. Collect the fraction story problems and create a class fraction book.	∙∙ ∙∙ ∙∙ ∙∙

For Groups That Finish Early

Extensions

- Have groups exchange fraction stories and discuss them.

Unit 2 Fractions: Parts and Wholes

Names

Do These Fraction Stories Make Sense?

Story 1: Johnny ordered a small pizza. The pizza maker asked him if he would like his pizza cut into 4 slices or 8 slices. Johnny thought for a minute and said, "Better make it 4 slices. I'm not hungry enough to eat 8 slices!" What do you think? Why?

Story 2: José came home from school one day and told his mother that he thinks he goes to school about $1/3$ of the days of each month. Is he right? How do you know?

Story 3: Juanita ran $2\,3/8$ miles. Tess ran $2\,2/5$ miles. After they finished running, Tess said that she had run closer to $2\,1/2$ miles than Juanita had. What do you think? How do you know?

© Addison-Wesley Publishing Company, Inc. Unit 2, Lesson 10: What Do You Think? Group Record Sheet

UNIT 3 Overview

Large Numbers

Mathematical Development

This unit provides opportunities for students to think about large numbers. Students explore place value concepts using concrete objects and calculators, investigate large numbers in real-world contexts, and write about their understanding of large numbers. Developmentally, this unit may be more appropriate for students in the second half of the school year.

Lesson 1 is a team builder that helps students find things they have in common. In Lesson 2, students continue to develop their sense of the magnitude of large numbers as they investigate and make reasonable estimates of numbers in the real world. In Lessons 3, 6, and 7, students begin to generalize about the organizational structure of our place value system as they compose and decompose numbers on their calculators and explore place value concepts in games involving large sums of play-money. In Lessons 4 and 5, students describe and compare the magnitude of large numbers and use logical reasoning to guess a number. In Lesson 8, students express appreciation to their partner for their work together.

Social Development

The focus of this unit is to provide opportunities for students to take responsibility for their own learning and behavior. The unit also fosters communication skills such as listening, asking questions, and checking for understanding and agreement. Open-ended questions help students examine how the underlying values of fairness, caring, and responsibility relate to behavior, and how their behavior affects group work and interaction. Students reflect on their group interaction, discuss problems, and suggest other ways to work.

Students work in randomly formed pairs that stay together throughout the unit; in Lessons 3 and 6, two pairs work together as a group of four.

Mathematical Emphasis

The experiences in this unit help students construct their understanding that

- Numbers can be used to describe quantities.
- The relative magnitude of numbers can be described.
- Our place value system is based on an organizational structure of grouping and regrouping.
- Numbers can be composed and decomposed.
- A problems may have more than one solution and may be solved in a variety of ways.
- Making a reasonable estimate requires gathering and using information.
- Logical reasoning can be used to solve problems.

Social Emphasis

Socially, experiences in this unit help students to

- Develop appropriate group skills.
- Take responsibility for learning and behavior.
- Analyze the effect of behavior on others and on the group work.
- Relate the values of fairness, caring, and responsibility to behavior.

Overview

Lessons

This unit includes eight lessons, plus an ongoing bulletin board activity. The calendar icon indicates some preparation is needed prior to that lesson.

1. **Find Someone Who…!**
   (page 137)
   Introductory team-building lesson that encourages cooperation between partners.

2. **What Makes Sense?**
   (page 143)
   Assessment lesson that provides information about your students' sense of the relative magnitude of large numbers.

3. **A Million Bucks 1**
   (page 147)
   Trading game in which groups of four gain experience grouping and regrouping hundreds, thousands, ten thousands, and hundred thousands.

4. **Facts About Numbers**
   (page 157)
   Ongoing activity in which pairs discuss and describe large numbers and their relative magnitude.

5. **Wipe Out**
   (page 161)
   Calculator lesson in which pairs compose and decompose large numbers.

6. **Guesswork**
   (page 171)
   Logical reasoning lesson in which groups of four discuss and describe large numbers and their relative magnitude.

7. **A Million Bucks 2**
   (page 177)
   Writing lesson in which pairs write about large numbers.

8. **Large-Number Buddies**
   (page 181)
   Transition lesson in which pairs reflect on their work together and thank each other.

"Large Numbers" Bulletin Board

Throughout this unit, ask students to collect examples of large numbers from newspaper and magazine articles and headlines and post these examples on a "Large Numbers" bulletin board. Frequently refer to the information in the clippings, and ask students to discuss such questions as whether they think the numbers are estimates or exact, whether the numbers seem reasonable, and how the numbers might have been derived.

Materials

Throughout the unit, students need access to supplies, such as scissors, pencils, markers, crayons, rulers, and glue sticks. If possible, each group should have a container with these supplies.

The materials needed for the unit are listed below. The first page of each lesson lists the materials specific to that lesson. All blackline masters for transparencies and group record sheets are included at the end of each lesson. Many of the materials are available in the *Number Power* Grade 4 Package.

Teacher Materials

- Bulletin board space for "Large Number" clippings
- Overhead projector and markers
- Transparency of "Find Someone Who…!" group record sheet (Lesson 1)
- Transparency of "What Makes Sense?" group record sheet (Lesson 2)
- Transparency of "A Million Bucks" trading mat (Lesson 3; optional)
- Transparency of "A Million Bucks" play-money (Lesson 3; optional)
- References, such as a world almanac, several copies if possible (Lesson 4)
- Sentence strips (Lesson 4)
- Catalogs and newspaper and magazine advertisements (Lesson 4 "Extensions")
- Calculator for the overhead projector, or an overhead transparency of a calculator (Lesson 5)
- Transparency of the "Make It Large" place value mat and 10 number cards (Lesson 5; optional)
- "Make It Large" place value mat and 10 number cards for each pair (Lesson 5 "Extensions")
- Slotted shoebox labeled "Class Mailbox" (Lesson 8)
- Chart paper and markers (Lesson 8)

Student Materials

Each student needs

- "Find Someone Who…!" group record sheet (Lesson 1)
- "A Million Bucks" trading mat (Lesson 3; Lesson 4 "Extensions;" Lesson 6 "Extensions;" Lesson 7 "Extensions")
- Envelope containing 10 each of the following "A Million Bucks" play-money bills: $100; $1,000; $10,000; $100,000 (Lesson 3; Lesson 4 "Extensions;" Lesson 6 "Extensions;" Lesson 7 "Extensions")
- Writing paper and a letter-size envelope (Lesson 8)

Each pair needs

- "What Makes Sense?" group record sheet (Lesson 2)
- Approximately 5 blank sentence strips (Lesson 4)
- Calculator (Lesson 5)

Each group of four needs

- 2 dice, one numbered 4-9 and one labeled $100; $1,000; $1,000; $10,000; $10,000; and $100,000 (Lesson 3; Lesson 4 "Extensions;" Lesson 6 "Extensions;" Lesson 7 "Extensions")
- "A Million Bucks" play-money million-dollar bill (Lesson 3; Lesson 4 "Extensions;" Lesson 6 "Extensions;" Lesson 7 "Extensions")
- Paper plate (Lesson 3; Lesson 4 "Extensions;" Lesson 6 "Extensions;" Lesson 7 "Extensions")
- Eight "Guesswork" 5-digit number cards (Lesson 6)

Teaching Hints

- Prior to each lesson, think about open-ended questions you might ask to extend and probe your students' thinking. Decide which "Extensions" to have ready when pairs or groups finish early.

- After each lesson, review any "Extensions" students have not explored and decide whether to have them investigate these "Extensions" before going on to the next lesson.

- Allow students time to freely explore unfamiliar or infrequently used materials before the lesson.

Assessment Techniques

The informal assessment techniques outlined below will help you determine your students' understanding of the relative magnitude of large numbers. Students' understanding will vary from experience to experience, particularly as they are beginning to construct their understanding. Some students may think it is reasonable for a million people to attend a professional baseball game or for the cost of a new car to be $500,000. Some students may have a better sense of the magnitude of large numbers, but may not be able to read or write them. These students, and probably most of the students in your class, will need many experiences encountering and investigating large numbers and linking their understanding to place value concepts.

The assessment questions suggested here and in the lessons can help you determine what students seem to understand and what further experiences to provide. Prior to each lesson, prepare possible questions to ask yourself or the students to help you assess students' understanding of large numbers. Accept student responses to your questions without a judgmental reaction. When appropriate, ask follow-up questions to more deeply probe their thinking.

Observe Individual Students Working with Large Numbers

As students work, observe individuals and ask yourself the questions below.

> **Q. Does the student have a sense of the relative magnitude of large numbers (size, capacity, distance, cost, etc.)?**

Note: Students need many opportunities to discuss and experience large numbers in context before they develop a sense of their magnitude. Such activities as finding and discussing examples of large numbers in newspapers and magazines or determining the relationship of one number to another (for example, is it larger or smaller? about half? almost the same?) help students develop an understanding of large numbers.

> **Q. Can the student read and write large numbers?**

Note: Students might be able to write large numbers but not be able to read them, or vice versa. Students need opportunities to work with concrete materials that help them recognize not only the value of each place but also the value of the periods within a number. (For example, the following illustrates period values: 346 in 346,702 is read as three-hundred forty-six thousand, while 346 in 346,702,013 is read as three-hundred forty-six million.) Such games and activities as A Million Bucks and Wipe Out will help students become familiar with the names for place values and period values.

Student Writing

Throughout the unit, ask students to verbalize their thinking, and, at times, to explain their thinking in writing. During this unit, students write about

- The magnitude, quantity, and place value of large numbers.
- Their understanding of large numbers.
- Their appreciation for their partners.

UNIT 3 Large Numbers

Lesson 1

Find Someone Who...!

Students survey some of their classmates and record their findings on their "Find Someone Who...!" group record sheet. Students form pairs with whomever they are talking to when you call "time."

Team Builder Emphasis
In this lesson, students

- Find things in common with their classmates.
- Develop a sense of identity as a pair.

Social Emphasis
In this lesson, students

- Listen to others.
- Ask questions to get information.

Students continue to

- Develop appropriate group skills.
- Take responsibility for learning and behavior.

Group Size: 2

Teacher Materials

- Transparency of "Find Someone Who...!" group record sheet

Student Materials
Each student needs

- "Find Someone Who...!" group record sheet
- Pencil

Lesson 1 Find Someone Who...! 137

Before the Lesson

- You may wish to personalize the survey questions for your class by having students generate a list of things they like and making your own "Find Someone Who...!" group record sheet.

Notes	Teacher	Students
	Introduce the lesson by discussing some of your favorite things with the class, for example, your favorite movie, flavor of ice cream, or your favorite color. Ask if anybody likes the same flavor of ice cream, then facilitate a discussion about how finding things in common with someone can affect how you relate to that person.	
	Show the "Find Someone Who...!" transparency. Ask students to think about and list their favorite movie, sport, flavor of ice cream, musical group, and color.	Students individually list their favorite for each category on the "Find Someone Who...!" group record sheet.
Ask two students to demonstrate how they would ask each other the survey questions. Discuss respectful ways to interact, such as making eye contact, using each other's names, and thanking each other before going on to another student. Ask students how they can be responsible for monitoring the noise level.	Explain that for each category, students will try to find at least two classmates who have the same choice. Discuss how to ask survey questions and how to record on the "Find Someone Who...!" group record sheet. Q. How do you feel about sharing information about yourself? Q. How can you show that you are listening to someone?	

138   Unit 3   Large Numbers

Notes	Teacher	Students
	Have students survey as many classmates as possible and write students' names in the appropriate categories on the group record sheet. After approximately 10 minutes, give students a signal to stop. Ask students to sit with the classmate with whom they are talking, and explain that these pairs will work together throughout this unit as they investigate large numbers.	• Individually, students 1. Ask each other survey questions to find for each category at least two students who have the same favorites. 2. Write the interviewed students' names next to the appropriate categories on their group record sheet. 3. Sit with the classmate they are surveying when the teacher calls "time."
	Ask pairs to discuss the categories on their group record sheets and add their names to their partner's sheet, if they have any of the same favorites. Have them discuss the things they have in common and decide on a name for their pair that reflects a common interest.	•• In pairs, students 1. Discuss the categories on the group record sheets and add their names to their partner's sheet, if they have any of the same favorites. 2. Discuss the things they might have in common. 3. Decide on a group name that reflects something they have in common.
	Have pairs share why they chose their group name and what they have in common. Help students reflect on the lesson by asking questions, such as: **Q. Was it difficult to find classmates to fit each of the categories? Why?**	•• •• •• ••

Lesson 1   Find Someone Who…!   139

Notes	Teacher	Students
	Q. Was it easy or hard to find interests you and your partner have in common? Why?	•• •• •• ••
Social Emphasis Take responsibility for learning and behavior.	Q. How were you responsible? Q. What would you do differently or the same the next time you work with your partner?	

Extensions

For Pairs That Finish Early

- Have pairs discuss their families and what their families might have in common.

For the Next Day

- Have pairs write their own survey, ask other pairs the survey questions, and report the results.

Names

Find Someone Who…!

Directions: List your favorite for each category. Find at least two classmates for each category who have the same favorite you do. Write their names.

My favorite movie   Names of classmates
_____   _____
                                     _____

My favorite sport to play   Names of classmates
_____   _____
                                     _____

My favorite flavor of ice cream   Names of classmates
_____   _____
                                     _____

My favorite music group   Names of classmates
_____   _____
                                     _____

My favorite color   Names of classmates
_____   _____
                                     _____

UNIT 3 Large Numbers

Lesson 2

What Makes Sense?

Students consider the magnitude of numbers as they discuss numbers that make sense for specific situations.

1 DAYS AHEAD

ASSESSMENT

Mathematical Emphasis

In this lesson, students

- Make reasonable estimates.

Students add to their understanding that

- Making a reasonable estimate requires gathering and using information.
- The relative magnitude of numbers can be described.
- Numbers can be used to describe quantities.

Social Emphasis

In this lesson, students

- Explain their thinking.
- Check for agreement.

Students continue to

- Develop appropriate group skills.
- Analyze the effect of behavior on others and on the group work.
- Take responsibility for learning and behavior.

Group Size: 2

Teacher Materials

- Overhead projector and markers
- Transparency of "What Makes Sense?" group record sheet

Student Materials

Each pair needs

- "What Makes Sense?" group record sheet
- Pencil

Lesson 2 What Makes Sense? 143

Before the Lesson

- Explain that students will explore large numbers during the next few weeks. Ask students to collect examples of large numbers from newspaper and magazine articles and headlines that will be posted on a bulletin board and discussed during the unit.

- You may wish to change the questions on the "What Makes Sense?" group record sheet to reflect your students' experiences.

Notes	Teacher	Students
This lesson provides opportunities to assess students' understanding of large numbers. Its purpose is not to determine mastery. Students will demonstrate different levels of sophistication concerning large numbers. Throughout this unit, opportunities for continued assessment will be noted. See "Assessment Techniques" in the Overview (p. 134) for additional ideas.	Lead a discussion about when large numbers are used. Show the "What Makes Sense?" transparency on the overhead projector and introduce the lesson. Explain that pairs will discuss and choose reasonable estimates for the statements on the "What Makes Sense?" group record sheet, then write two problems of their own. Facilitate a discussion about how pairs might help each other and why it is important for students to explain their thinking and to check for agreement. Ask questions, such as: Q. Why is it important to give reasons for your opinion? Q. How might you check to see that you both agree to your choices? Why is that important?	•• •• •• ••
Resist the urge to help students make estimates. Observe students, and ask yourself what indications you see that: ■ Students have sufficient knowledge and experience to make a reasonable estimate. ■ Students have a sense of the relative magnitude of large numbers.	**O**bserve students, and ask questions, such as: Q. Why do you think this estimate is reasonable? Q. How are you making decisions?	•• In pairs, students 1. Discuss the situations on the group record sheet and choose a reasonable estimate. 2. Write two problems of their own.

Notes	Teacher	Students
Mathematical Emphasis Making a reasonable estimate requires gathering and using information.	As a class, discuss questions, such as: Q. What did you estimate? How did you choose that estimate? What helped you? Q. Was it difficult to make an estimate for some questions? Which ones? Why? Which were easier? Why?	•• •• •• ••

Help students recognize that many factors can affect the reasonableness of their estimates, such as the size of the movie theater or concert arena and the type of car. There may be several reasonable estimates for each statement.

Q. Did any pair choose another estimate? Why?

Have several pairs share their problems with the class. First in pairs, then as a class, have students discuss estimates for the problems generated by the pairs.

Help students reflect on their work by asking questions, such as:

Social Emphasis Take responsibility for learning and behavior.

Q. What did you like about the way you and your partner worked?

Q. What problems did you and your partner have? How did you solve them? How might you avoid those problems next time?

Ask students to continue to collect examples of large numbers from newspaper and magazine articles and headlines for the "Large Numbers" bulletin board.

Extensions

For Pairs That Finish Early

- Ask pairs to compare the numbers on the group record sheet. Have pairs write about the relationships they notice. For example, 6,000 is ten times larger than 600.

For the Next Day

- Have students contribute the articles and headlines they found to the "Large Numbers" bulletin board. Ask students to speculate about whether the numbers they found are estimates or exact. Encourage students to justify their thinking.

Lesson 2   What Makes Sense?

Names
_____

What Makes Sense?

Discuss each problem, and together choose what you think is a reasonable estimate. Be prepared to explain the reasons for your choice.

1. We have about _____ students in our school.

    50,000   5,000   500

2. It costs about _____ for a new car.

    $200,000 $20,000 $2,000

3. About _____ fans might attend a rock concert.

    60,000   6,000   600

4. About _____ people might be in a movie theater on a Saturday night.

    40,000   4,000   400

Write one or two problems for the class to discuss.

1.

2.

Unit 3, Lesson 2: What Makes Sense?   Group Record Sheet   © Addison-Wesley Publishing Company, Inc.

UNIT 3 Large Numbers

Lesson 3
A Million Bucks 1

Class set made & available for check out from RC

Students mentally compose and decompose numbers as they play a trading game.

DAYS AHEAD: 2

Mathematical Emphasis

In this lesson, students

- Regroup hundreds, thousands, ten thousands, and hundred thousands.

Students add to their understanding that

- Numbers can be composed and decomposed.
- Our place value system is based on an organizational structure of grouping and regrouping.

Social Emphasis

In this lesson, students

- Give help when needed.
- Agree before trading.

Students continue to

- Develop appropriate group skills.
- Take responsibility for learning and behavior.
- Analyze the effect of behavior on others and on the group work.

Group Size: 4

Teacher Materials

- Overhead projector
- Transparencies of "A Million Bucks" trading mat and play-money (optional)

Student Materials

Each student needs

- "A Million Bucks" trading mat (see "Before the Lesson")
- Envelope containing "A Million Bucks" play-money bills (see "Before the Lesson")

Each group of four needs

- 2 special dice (see "Before the Lesson")
- "A Million Bucks" play-money million-dollar bill (see "Before the Lesson")
- "Pot" (a paper plate)

Lesson 2   A Million Bucks 1

Before the Lesson

- For each student, prepare a trading mat by copying the blackline master and taping the two halves together. Also copy the play-money blackline master and cut into bills. Put ten of each of the following denominations into an envelope for each student: $100; $1,000; $10,000; and $100,000. Copy and cut one "A Million Bucks" million-dollar bill for each group.

- Make two dice for each group, one numbered 4 to 9 and one labeled $100; $1,000; $1,000; $10,000; $10,000; and $100,000. Write the numbers on adhesive dots and place the dots on the dice, or purchase blank dice and labels at a supply store. Make a transparency of the trading mat and play-money bills using the blackline masters (optional).

- Familiarize yourself with the game before introducing it to the class. Note possible strategies students might use when they trade bills.

Notes	Teacher	Students
	Introduce the lesson and ask:	
	Q. What would you do if you had a million dollars?	
	State that groups will play a game called A Million Bucks and explain these rules:	
Consider showing the trading mat on an overhead projector and demonstrating how to play the game. Emphasize the importance of	1. The goal of the game is for the group to have a million-dollar bill in their "pot."	
■ Reading the amount of money on the trading mat. ■ Organizing and keeping track of materials. ■ Working cooperatively to get a million dollars in the group's "pot."	2. Each student, in turn, rolls two dice, and takes from his or her envelope the amount of money indicated by the dice. (For example, if a student rolls 4 and $1,000, he or she takes four $1,000 bills from their envelope.) The student then places this money on his or her trading mat, and reads aloud the total amount on the mat.	
	3. When a student has ten 100s, 1,000s, or 10,000s, he or she must trade them for a bill of the next denomination. All group members must agree that the trade is appropriate. After the trade, the student again reads aloud the total on his or her mat.	
	4. Whenever a student gets $100,000, he or she puts the $100,000 bill in the "pot."	
	5. The group keeps track of the amount of money in the "pot." When they have ten $100,000 bills, they trade them for the million-dollar bill.	

148   Unit 3   Large Numbers

Notes	Teacher	Students
	Explain that in 1969 the government stopped printing denominations of $500 and higher; however, denominations of $500, $1,000, $5,000, and $10,000 are still in circulation, although $5,000 and $10,000 bills are considered rare. State that, for the purposes of this game, students will use $100,000 bills and $1,000,000 bills, although these do not actually exist in our currency.	∷ ∷ ∷ ∷
Social Emphasis Take responsibility for learning and behavior.	Facilitate a discussion about ways to work cooperatively. Ask questions, such as: Q. If you need help deciding how to make a trade, what might you say? Q. How could you give help trading without actually doing it for someone? What could you say? Q. Why is it important that you make sure all members of the group agree before trading?	
Mathematical Emphasis Our place value system is based on an organizational structure of grouping and regrouping.	**O**bserve groups playing the game. Ask questions, such as: Q. How much money do you have? Q. How many 100s equal one thousand? How many 1,000s equal ten thousand? How many 10,000s equal one hundred thousand? How many 100,000s equal one million? Q. How are you checking that you all agree to a trade? Q. How did you make that trade?	∷ In groups, students 1. Take turns playing the game. 2. Agree to each trade and help each other with trades.
Social Emphasis Analyze the effect of behavior on others and on the group work.	If groups are having difficulty working together, ask questions, such as: Q. What is the problem? What needs to be different? Q. How is your work affected by your group's behavior? Q. What have you tried? What else could you try?	

Lesson 3 A Million Bucks 1

| **Notes** | **Teacher** | **Students** |

Help the class reflect on the activity by asking questions, such as:

Q. How much money did your group have in its "pot" at the end of the game? How much more money would your group need to be able to trade for a million-dollar bill? How do you know?

Q. Why do you think we played this game?

Q. How did you help each other?

Q. What did you like about the way your group worked?

Q. What problems did your group have working together? How did you solve them?

Social Emphasis
Develop appropriate group skills.

Extensions

For Groups That Finish Early

- Have groups play the game again, as they will benefit from playing this game many times. Ask questions to help students focus on the mathematics involved.

For the Next Day

- Have the game available for groups to play when they have free time, or play the game as a class activity.

- Have students contribute articles and headlines to the "Large Numbers" bulletin board. Ask students to speculate on how the numbers in the articles might have been derived.

A Million Bucks!
Overhead Trading Mat

$100,000	$10,000	$1,000	$100

A Million
Student

$100,000 $10,000

Bucks!
Trading Mat

$1,000	$100

For use on the overhead projector. Make a transparency and cut apart.

$1,000,000,000	$1,000,000,000	$1,000,000,000
$100,000	$100,000	$100,000
$10,000	$10,000	$10,000
$1,000	$1,000	$1,000
$100	$100	$100
$100,000	$100,000	$100,000
$10,000	$10,000	$10,000
$1,000	$1,000	$1,000
$100	$100	$100

$100	$100
$1,000	$1,000
$10,000	$10,000
$100,000	$100,000

$1,000,000	$1,000,000
$1,000,000	$1,000,000
$1,000,000	$1,000,000
$1,000,000	$1,000,000

UNIT 3 Large Numbers

Lesson 4

Facts About Numbers

This lesson introduces an ongoing class activity. A large number is displayed and every few days, students write and discuss statements about the number.

Mathematical Emphasis

In this lesson, students

- Use comparisons to describe large numbers.

Students add to their understanding that

- Numbers can be used to describe quantities.
- The relative magnitude of numbers can be described.

Social Emphasis

In this lesson, students

- Explain their thinking.
- Check for understanding.

Students continue to

- Develop appropriate group skills.
- Take responsibility for learning and behavior.

Group Size: 2

Teacher Materials

- A place to display sentence strips on the "Large Numbers" bulletin board
- References that include large numbers, such as a world almanac
- 2 sentence strips
- Extra sentence strips for ongoing activity
- Catalogs and advertisements for "Extensions"
- "A Million Bucks" game materials for "Extensions"

Student Materials

Each pair needs

- Approximately 5 blank sentence strips
- Markers

Lesson 4 Facts About Numbers

157

Notes	Teacher	Students
	Briefly introduce the lesson and explain that you will periodically post a 5- or 6-digit number taken from the articles and headlines on the "Large Numbers" bulletin board and that pairs will write statements about the number.	•• •• •• ••
Mathematical Emphasis The relative magnitude of numbers can be described.	Find a number on the "Large Numbers" bulletin board, such as 50,264, write it on a sentence strip, and post it. Ask questions, such as: Q. **What can you say about 50,264?** Q. **How does 50,264 relate to 100,000? What statement can you make about that relationship? Other statements?**	
At first, students might have difficulty generating statements about the number. You may want to discuss some examples as a class, such as: ■ 50,264 is a little more than 50,000. ■ 50,264 is about half of 100,000. ■ 50,264 is about the same as the cost of a luxury automobile. ■ 50,264 is about the same as the population of a small city in the United States of America.	Discuss the available references (such as a world almanac or the Guinness Book of World Records) that might help students write statements. Facilitate a discussion about how students might help each other. Ask students to discuss why it is important for them to explain their thinking and check for understanding.	
	As pairs write statements about the number, ask questions, such as: Q. **What do you know about 50,264?** Q. **How are you making decisions about what to write?** Q. **How do you know this statement is true?**	•• In pairs, students generate, discuss, and write statements about a large number.

Notes	Teacher	Students
	Have pairs post their statements. Point to statements and ask questions, such as:	•• •• •• ••
	Q. Do you agree with this statement? Why or why not?	
	Q. What resource was used to verify this statement?	
Social Emphasis Develop appropriate group skills.	Help students reflect on their work by asking questions, such as:	•• •• •• ••
	Q. How did it help you to have a partner today?	
	Q. What problems did you have working together? What will you do differently next time?	
	Explain that you will post a new number on the bulletin board every few days and that pairs will have time to write statements about the number.	
	Find a new number on the "Large Numbers" bulletin board, write it on a sentence strip, and post it.	
	Encourage pairs to discuss the number with their families and to use references, such as a world almanac, to help generate ideas.	
	On succeeding days, provide opportunities for students to continue the activity.	

Lesson 4   Facts About Numbers

Extensions

For Pairs That Finish Early
- Have pairs write statements about the number one million.
- Have students play A Million Bucks.

For the Next Day
- Provide catalogs and advertisements from the real estate, automobile, and travel sections of the newspaper. Ask pairs to decide what they would buy from the catalogs and ads if they could spend one million dollars. Have pairs

  1. Agree on each purchase.
  2. List all purchases.
  3. Spend as close to one million dollars as possible without spending more than one million dollars.

- Have students contribute articles and headlines to the "Large Numbers" bulletin board. Ask students to speculate on whether the numbers are estimates or exact and encourage students to justify their thinking.

UNIT 3 Large Numbers
Wipe Out

Lesson 5

Students play a game with a calculator. Partners take turns entering a 4-, 5-, or 6-digit number in their calculator and then try to wipe out one of the digits without clearing the calculator.

Mathematical Emphasis

In this lesson, students

- Use a calculator to add and subtract.
- Mentally add and subtract.

Students add to their understanding that

- Numbers can be composed and decomposed.
- Problems may have more than one solution and may be solved in a variety of ways.
- Our place value system is based on an organizational structure of grouping and regrouping.

Social Emphasis

In this lesson, students

- Check for understanding.
- Share the work in a fair way.

Students continue to

- Develop appropriate group skills.
- Take responsibility for learning and behavior.

Group Size: 2

Teacher Materials

- Calculator for the overhead projector or an overhead transparency of a calculator similar to students' calculators
- Overhead projector and markers
- Transparency of the "Make It Large" place value mat and 10 number cards for "Extensions" (optional; see "Before the Lesson")
- "Make It Large" place value mat and 10 number cards for each pair for "Extensions" (see "Before the Lesson")

Student Materials

Each pair needs

- Calculator

Lesson 5   Wipe Out

161

Before the Lesson

- If students have had little previous experience using a calculator, provide opportunities for them to explore its use.

- For "Extensions," prepare a place value mat for each student by copying the two "Make It Large" blackline masters and taping the two halves together. Copy the number cards and cut apart.

- Also for "Extensions," make a transparency of the "Make It Large" place value mat and the 10 number cards from the blackline masters to demonstrate the game Make It Large (optional). You will need a set of student cards for playing the game.

Notes

Mathematical Emphasis
Numbers can be composed and decomposed.

As they demonstrate, ask students to explain their thinking on the overhead projector calculator.

Consider modeling the game by demonstrating it with a student partner.

Teacher

Briefly introduce the lesson and explain that pairs will continue to explore large numbers by playing a calculator game called Wipe Out.

Begin with a practice example. Ask pairs to display 5,926 on their calculators. Have partners read the number to each other. Then ask pairs to "wipe out" (change to zero) the 9 in 5,926 without clearing the calculator and without using a 9. Ask questions, such as:

Q. What strategy did you and your partner use to wipe out the 9? Other strategies?

Q. What did you and your partner do that helped you work cooperatively to solve this problem?

Repeat this activity four or five times with 4-, 5-, and 6-digit numbers. Ask pairs to share their strategies.

Explain how to play the game Wipe Out.

1. Partner A enters a 4-, 5-, or 6-digit number into the calculator and reads the number to partner B.

2. Partner A gives the calculator to partner B and tells him or her which digit to wipe out.

3. Partner B wipes out the digit without clearing the calculator or using the same digit they are wiping out and explains the process to partner A.

Students

• •   • •

• •   • •

Unit 3   Large Numbers

Notes	Teacher	Students
	4. Partners switch roles and play again.	•• ••
	5. Pairs play the game several times.	•• ••
Social Emphasis Take responsibility for learning and behavior.	Facilitate a discussion about the cooperative behaviors that might help students play the game. Ask questions, such as: Q. What might you and your partner do to make sure you both understand the strategy you used to wipe out a number? Why is this important?	•• •• •• ••
	As students play the game, ask questions, such as: Q. What strategies are working for you? Q. How are you making sure you both understand the strategies?	•• In pairs, students play the game, switching roles for each game.
Mathematical Emphasis Problems may have more than one solution and may be solved in a variety of ways. Students might use strategies such as: ■ Subtract 600 from 4,705 and 100 from 4,105. ■ Subtract 100 seven times from 4,705. ■ Multiply 9 times 4,705, subtract 300, and subtract 38,040. ■ Divide 4,705 by 5 and add 3,064. To stimulate student thinking, consider sharing a strategy of your own with the class.	Have several pairs share their strategies with the class. Ask questions, such as: Q. What strategies did you use to wipe out the digits? Other strategies? Ask pairs to display 4,705 on their calculators. First in pairs, then as a class, have students discuss and find several strategies for changing the 7 to zero without clearing the calculator and without using 7. Ask several pairs to explain their strategies to the class. Have pairs try each other's strategies and discuss whether they agree with the strategy.	•• •• •• ••

Lesson 5 Wipe Out

Notes	Teacher	Students

Help students reflect on the activity by asking questions, such as:

Q. What new strategies did you learn?

Q. What new information about large numbers did you learn from playing this game?

Q. What did you like about the way you and your partner worked?

To help students develop an understanding of the relative magnitude of large numbers, have pairs investigate the activity listed in "Extensions for the Next Day" before going on to the next lesson.

Extensions

For Pairs That Finish Early

- Ask pairs to choose and write about one of the strategies they used to wipe out a digit on their calculator.

For the Next Day

- As a class, play Make It Large. Each pair needs a place value mat and ten cards, each with a different single-digit number made from the blackline master (see "Before the Lesson"). You need an identical set of cards. (You may also wish to have a transparency of the game board and cards to demonstrate the game.) The object of this game is to make the largest 6-digit number possible.

    1. Draw a card.
    2. Read the number on the card.
    3. Ask pairs to place their matching card on their place value mat in a way that will help them to make the largest number possible. (Pairs can not move the card once they have placed it on their mat.)
    4. Continue play until six numbers have been drawn and read to the class, then discuss the numbers pairs have made.

Make It Large
Overhead Place Value Mat

Hundred Thousands	Ten Thousands	Thousands	Hundreds	Tens	Ones

Make It
Student Place

Hundred Thousands	Ten Thousands	Thousands

Large
Value Mat

Hundreds	Tens	Ones

For use on the overhead projector. Make a transparency and cut apart.

0	1	2	3	4	5	6	7	8	9
0	1	2	3	4	5	6	7	8	9
0	1	2	3	4	5	6	7	8	9
0	1	2	3	4	5	6	7	8	9

4	9
3	8
2	7
1	6
0	5

UNIT 3 Large Numbers

Lesson 6

Guesswork

Students use logical thinking and their understanding of large numbers to play a number-guessing game.

Mathematical Emphasis

In this lesson, students

- Ask logical questions.
- Compare and order numbers.

Students add to their understanding that

- The relative magnitude of numbers can be described.
- A problem may have more than one solution and may be solved in a variety of ways.
- Logical reasoning can be used to solve problems.

Social Emphasis

In this lesson, students

- Ask questions to get information.
- Listen to others.
- Give accurate information.

Students continue to

- Develop appropriate group skills.
- Take responsibility for learning and behavior.

Group Size: 4

Teacher Materials

- "A Million Bucks" game materials for "Extensions"

Student Materials

Each group of four needs

- 8 "Guesswork" five-digit number cards (see "Before the Lesson")
- Paper and pencil

Before the Lesson

- For each group of students, copy and cut the eight number cards (see the blackline master).

Teacher

Introduce the lesson. First in groups, then as a class, discuss questions, such as:

Q. What types of guessing games have you enjoyed playing?

Q. Why do you like to play those games?

Explain that groups will use logical thinking and what they know about large numbers to play a guessing game. State that the object of the game is for one pair to guess a hidden number by asking specific questions that can be answered yes or no, and for the other pair to listen carefully to the questions and to give accurate information. Model playing the game:

1. Choose a student to be your partner and two students to be the other pair.

2. With your partner, face away from the class. Have the other pair choose one of the playing cards (for example, the card might say 39,022) and show the class the number printed on the card. Remind all students that they are not to say what is written on the card.

3. With your partner, discuss aloud and agree on the question to ask first. (For example, is the number larger than 50,000? larger than 25,000? smaller than 37,500?)

4. Have the other pair discuss your question aloud and decide whether to answer yes or no.

5. With your partner, discuss their answer aloud and decide on the next question to ask. Keep a record of the numbers discussed, such as that shown on the left.

6. Continue until you and your partner guess the number.

Students

∷ ∷
∷ ∷

Notes

larger than	smaller than
25,000 37,500	50,000

Discuss with the class how recording might help them keep track of the numbers.

172   Unit 3   Large Numbers

Notes	Teacher	Students
Social Emphasis Take responsibility for learning and behavior.	Facilitate a discussion about the importance of discussing and agreeing on the questions and answers, and of listening and responding accurately. Ask pairs to suggest ways to monitor the noise level during this activity.	
If students have trouble working with each other, open-ended questions may help them analyze the effect of the behaviors that are causing difficulty. Ask questions, such as: Q. What seems to be causing problems? Q. What might you do about that? Q. How might that help? How is that a fair way to work?	Observe groups working and, when appropriate, ask questions, such as: Q. What strategy are you using to guess the number? Q. How are you and your partner agreeing on the questions you are going to ask?	∷ In groups of four, students play the game, with pairs switching roles after each game.
Mathematical Emphasis The relative magnitude of numbers can be described.	First in groups, then as a class, ask questions, such as: Q. Is 20,678 closer to 20,000 or 30,000? Why? Q. Is 48,805 closer to 40,000 or 50,000? Why? Q. Is 39,022 closer to 39,000 or 40,000? Why? Q. Is 85,250 closer to 85,000 or 86,000? Why? Q. What are some numbers close to 99,999?	∷ ∷ ∷ ∷

Lesson 6   Guesswork

Notes

Provide several opportunities for students to play the game before discussing it as a class.

Mathematical Emphasis

Logical reasoning can be used to solve problems.

Teacher

Help students reflect on the activity by asking questions, such as:

Q. **What helped you and your group work well together?**

Q. **What strategies helped you and your group guess the number?**

Q. **What strategies might help you guess the number with the fewest questions possible?**

Students

▶▶▶

For Groups That Finish Early

For the Next Day

Extensions

- Have groups play A Million Bucks.

- Have pairs make up cards for each other and play the game again.

- Ask students to find numbers on the "Large Numbers" bulletin board that use decimals. First in pairs, then as a class, discuss the meaning of the numbers. (For example, 29.9 million means that it is almost 30 million.) Ask students to speculate on whether numbers are estimates or exact.

20,678	39,022
48,805	56,780
61,500	74,113
85,250	99,999

UNIT 3 Large Numbers

Lesson 7

A Million Bucks 2

Students write what they learned about large numbers after playing A Million Bucks. The whole class discusses large numbers.

DAYS AHEAD 5

Mathematical Emphasis

In this lesson, students

- Write about large numbers.
- Compute mentally.

Students add to their understanding that

- The relative magnitude of numbers can be described.
- Numbers can be composed and decomposed.
- Our place value system is based on an organizational structure of grouping and regrouping.

Social Emphasis

In this lesson, students

- Discuss thinking before writing.
- Check for understanding.

Students continue to

- Develop appropriate group skills.
- Take responsibility for learning and behavior.

Group Size: 2

Teacher Materials

- "A Million Bucks" game materials (see "Before the Lesson" and "Extensions")

Student Materials

Each pair needs

- Paper and pencil

Lesson 7   A Million Bucks 2   177

Before the Lesson

- Students should be given many opportunities over a span of many days to play and discuss "A Million Bucks" (Lesson 3) before they are asked to generalize about large numbers.

Notes	Teacher	Students

Mathematical Emphasis

Numbers can be composed and decomposed.

Discuss concepts fostered by playing A Million Bucks by asking questions, such as:

Q. How many 100s equal one thousand? How many 1,000s equal ten thousand? How many 10,000s equal one hundred thousand? How many 100,000s equal one million?

Q. If you wanted to trade $3,900 for $100 bills, how many $100 bills would you get? How do you know?

Q. If you have $45,000, how much more do you need before you can trade for $100,000? How do you know?

Ask two students to each write a 5-digit number on the board. As a class, compare the two numbers by discussing questions, such as:

Q. Which one is closer to 10,000? How do you know?

Q. Are these numbers closer to 15,000 or to 20,000? Why?

Have several more pairs generate sets of five-digit numbers. Ask questions that help students explore the relative magnitude of the two numbers in each set.

The class may need to brainstorm a few ideas before pairs start writing. If students are not ready to generalize in writing about large numbers, consider having pairs only discuss what they learned about large numbers from playing the game A Million Bucks.

Ask pairs to discuss and write about what they learned about large numbers when playing the game A Million Bucks.

•• ••

•• ••

178   Unit 3   Large Numbers

Notes	Teacher	Students
Social Emphasis Develop appropriate group skills.	Facilitate a discussion about what might help pairs work well. Specifically discuss the need for partners to discuss their thinking before writing and to check for understanding. Ask questions, such as: Q. Why is it important to discuss your thinking before you write? Q. How might you check your partner's understanding of your thinking? Your own understanding of your partner's thinking?	•• •• •• ••

As you observe, ask yourself questions, such as: ■ Does the student understand place value concepts? Does the student understand that ten 100s regroup to 1,000; ten 1,000s regroup to 10,000; and so on? ■ How does the student explain his or her thinking processes? ■ Does the student compute mentally? ■ Does the student have a sense of the relative magnitude of a given large number? See "Assessment Techniques" in the Overview (p. 134) for other suggestions.	**O**bserve students working and, when appropriate, ask questions, such as: Q. What else did you learn about large numbers when playing the game? Q. What number patterns did you notice? Q. What do you like about the way you and your partner are working?	•• In pairs, students write what they learned about large numbers when playing A Million Bucks.

Notes	Teacher	Students
	Ask several pairs to share what they learned about large numbers. Discuss statements made by the pairs and check for agreement on the part of the class. Ask students to explain why they agree or disagree.	•• •• •• ••
Social Emphasis Take responsibility for learning and behavior.	Help students reflect on their group work by asking questions, such as: Q. How did you check each other's understanding? Q. What did you like about the way you and your partner worked? Q. What problems did you and your partner have? How might you avoid those problems next time?	

▶▶▶ **Extensions**

For Pairs That Finish Early

- Have pairs play Write This Number. Ask pairs to take turns stating large numbers between 1,000 and 1,000,000 and writing those numbers. (For example, one partner might say "fifty-two thousand, five hundred eighteen," and the other partner would write 52,518.)

For the Next Day

- Have groups of four play a different version of A Million Bucks, in which each student starts with $100,000 and trades backward every time he or she rolls the dice. For example, if a student rolls a 5 and a 10,000, he or she trades in the $100,000 bill for ten $10,000 bills and puts five $10,000 bills in the pot, leaving $50,000 on his or her trading mat. The goal of the game is for the group to have $400,000 in the pot.

- Ask students to find numbers on the "Large Numbers" bulletin board that use decimals. First in pairs, then as a class, discuss numbers the example is close to and numbers it is between. For example, 5.3 million is close to 5 million and between 5 million and 6 million.

UNIT 3 Large Numbers

Lesson 8

Large-Number Buddies

Students individually write and "mail" a thank-you letter to their partner. In pairs, students discuss their favorite activities in the unit and what they liked about working together.

Transition Emphasis
In this lesson, students
- Reflect on how they worked together.
- Talk about what they learned about working together that will help them in other groups.
- Celebrate their successes and thank each other.
- Write a thank-you letter.

Social Emphasis
In this lesson, students
- Show appreciation for each other.
- Express feelings about working together.

Students continue to
- Develop appropriate group skills.
- Analyze the effect of behavior on others and on the group work.
- Relate the values of fairness, caring, and responsibility to behavior.

Teacher Materials
- Slotted shoe box labeled "Class Mailbox" (see "Before the Lesson")
- Chart labeled "What to Include in Your Thank-You Letter" (see "Before the Lesson")
- Marker

Student Materials
Each student needs
- Writing paper and a letter-size envelope
- Pencil

Group Size: 2

Lesson 8   Large-Number Buddies

181

Before the Lesson

 1 DAY AHEAD

- Make and label the Class Mailbox. (A large shoe box works well.)
- Make a chart entitled "Things We Might Write in Our Thank-You Letters."

Notes	Teacher	Students
	Introduce the lesson by asking students if they have ever written or received a thank-you letter. Ask questions, such as:	•• •• •• ••
	Q. What are some reasons for writing a thank-you letter?	
	Q. How do you feel when you receive a thank-you letter?	
	Explain that students will write a thank-you letter to their partners to express appreciation for the way they worked together during this unit.	
Social Emphasis Analyze the effect of behavior on others and on the group work.	Help students reflect on their interaction during this unit by asking questions, such as:	
	Q. How have you and your partner helped each other during this unit?	
	Q. How did you share the work and materials fairly? How did this help you?	
	Q. How did you take responsibility for your own actions and learning during this unit?	
	Q. What do you appreciate about your partner?	
	Q. Why do you think it is important to thank your partner?	
	Q. What do you think your partner would appreciate hearing from you?	

Notes	Teacher	Students
If necessary, suggest that students might include the following: 1. How well you and your partner worked. 2. What you would do differently next time. 3. What you appreciate (like) about your partner. 4. Your favorite large-number activity.	**H**ave students brainstorm the kinds of things they might include in their thank-you letters. Write students' responses on the "Things We Might Write in Our Thank-You Letters" chart. Explain that each student will write a thank-you letter to his or her partner, address an envelope with their partner's name, and put the letter in the Class Mailbox.	•• •• •• ••
	Observe students working. If they are having difficulty writing their thank-you letter, suggest they refer to the "Things We Might Write" chart.	• Individually, students 1. Write thank-you letters to their partners. 2. Put the letter in an envelope, address it with their partner's name, and put it in the Class Mailbox.
Students may wish to share their thank-you letters with the class. Be sure both partners agree and choose to do so.	**D**eliver the mail to students, and give them a few minutes to read the thank-you letters from their partners. Ask questions, such as: Q. How did reading your letter make you feel? Q. What would you do again the next time you work with a partner? What would you do differently? Q. If your partner had not written you a thank-you letter, how might you know what he or she liked about working with you?	•

Lesson 8 Large-Number Buddies

Notes

Use a cooperative structure such as "Turn to Your Partner" (see p. xi) to provide opportunities for all students to be involved in the discussion.

Social Emphasis
Analyze the effect of behavior on others and on the group work.

For Students That Finish Early

Teacher

Help students reflect on the lesson by asking questions, such as:

Q. **What helped your partnership work well?**

Q **What caused problems? How did you resolve them?**

Q. **What will you want to remember for the next time you work with a partner or group?**

Extensions

- Have students write a letter to themselves, describing how they worked with their partner during this unit. Ask them to include how their own actions helped their pair work well, the problems they had, and how they would work with their next partner. Have students put their letter in an envelope and address it to themselves. Collect the letters and keep them for the next time students work with a partner. Deliver the letters to the students before they begin working with their new partners.

Students

•• ••

•• ••

Additional Reading

Mathematics Education

California State Department of Education. *Mathematics Framework for California Public Schools, Kindergarten Through Grade Twelve.* Sacramento, CA: California State Department of Education, 1992.

———. *Mathematics Model Curriculum Guide, Kindergarten Through Grade Eight.* Sacramento, CA: California State Department of Education, 1987.

Ginsberg, Herbert P. *The Development of Mathematical Thinking.* New York: Academic Press, 1983.

Kamii, Constance. *Number in Preschool and Kindergarten.* Washington, DC: National Association for the Education of Young Children (NAEYC), 1982.

———. *Young Children Reinvent Arithmetic.* New York: Teachers College Press, 1985.

———. *Young Children Continue to Reinvent Arithmetic,* 2nd Grade. New York: Teachers College Press, 1989.

Kamii, Constance, and Barbara A. Lewis. "Research into Practice: Constructive Learning and Teaching." *Arithmetic Teacher,* 38 (1990), pp. 34–35.

Labinowicz, Ed. *The Piaget Primer.* Reading, MA: Addison-Wesley Publishing Company, 1980.

———. *Learning from Children. New Beginnings for Teaching Numerical Thinking.* Menlo Park, CA: Addison-Wesley Publishing Company, 1985.

Mathematical Sciences Education Board. *Counting on You: Actions Supporting Mathematics Teaching Standards.* Washington, DC: National Academy Press, 1991.

———. *On the Shoulders of Giants.* National Research Council, Washington, DC: National Academy Press, 1990.

National Council of Teachers of Mathematics. *Measurement in School Mathematics.* 1976 Yearbook. Reston, VA: National Council of Teachers of Mathematics, 1976.

———. *Developing Computational Skills.* 1978 Yearbook. Reston, VA: National Council of Teachers of Mathematics, 1978.

———. *Applications in School Mathematics.* 1979 Yearbook. Reston, VA: National Council of Teachers of Mathematics, 1979.

———. *Teaching Statistics and Probability.* 1981 Yearbook. Reston, VA: National Council of Teachers of Mathematics, 1981.

———. *Estimation and Mental Computation.* 1986 Yearbook. Reston, VA: National Council of Teachers of Mathematics, 1986.

———. *Learning and Teaching Geometry, K Through 12.* 1987 Yearbook. Reston, VA: National Council of Teachers of Mathematics, 1987.

———. *The Ideas of Algebra, K Through 12.* 1988 Yearbook. Reston, VA: National Council of Teachers of Mathematics, 1988.

———. *Arithmetic Teacher,* 36 (1989). Special focus issue on number sense.

———. *Curriculum and Evaluation Standards for School Mathematics.* Reston, VA: National Council of Teachers of Mathematics, 1989.

———. *Curriculum and Evaluation Standards for School Mathematics Addenda Series, Grades K Through 6.* Reston, VA: National Council of Teachers of Mathematics, 1991.

———. *Curriculum and Evaluation Standards for School Mathematics Addenda Series, Grades 5 Through 8.* Reston, VA: National Council of Teachers of Mathematics, 1991.

———. *New Directions for Elementary School Mathematics.* 1989 Yearbook. Reston, VA: National Council of Teachers of Mathematics, 1989.

———. *Professional Standards for Teaching Mathematics.* Reston, VA: National Council of Teachers of Mathematics, 1991.

National Research Council. *Everybody Counts: A Report to the Nation on the Future of Mathematics Education.* Washington, DC: National Academy Press, 1989.

———. *Reshaping School Mathematics: A Philosophy and Framework for Curriculum.* Washington, DC: National Academy Press, 1990.

Sowder, Judith T., and Bonnie P. Schappelle, eds. *Establishing Foundations for Research on Number Sense and Related Topics: Report of a Conference.* San Diego, CA: Center for Research in Mathematics and Science Education, 1989.

Stenmark, Jean K. (ed). *Mathematics Assessment: Myths, Models, Good Questions, and Practical Suggestions.* Reston, VA: National Council of Teachers of Mathematics, 1991.

———. *Assessment Alternatives in Mathematics: An Overview of Assessment Techniques That Promote Learning.* Berkeley, CA: Lawrence Hall of Science, University of California, 1989.

Cooperative Learning and Moral Development

Artzt, Alice F., and Claire M. Newman. *How to Use Cooperative Learning in the Mathematics Class.* Reston, VA: National Council of Teachers of Mathematics, 1990.

Brandt, Ron (ed). *Cooperative Learning.* Educational Leadership, 1989–90, 47.

Brubacher, Mark, Ryder Payne, and Kemp Rickett. *Perspectives on Small Group Learning, Theory, and Practice.* New York: Rubicon Publishing Inc., 1990.

Cohen, Elizabeth G. *Designing Groupwork: Strategies for the Heterogenous Classroom.* New York, NY: Teachers College Press, 1986.

Davidson, Neil, ed. *Cooperative Learning in Mathematics: A Handbook for Teachers.* Menlo Park, CA: Addison-Wesley Publishing Co., 1990.

Johnson, David. W., et al. *Circles of Learning: Cooperation in the Classroom.* Alexandria, VA: Association for Supervision and Curriculum Development, 1986.

Kohlberg, Lawrence. "Moral Stages and Moralization: The Cognitive Developmental Approach." In *Moral Development and Behavior,* T. Lickona, ed. New York: Holt, Rinehart and Winston, 1976.

———. *The Psychology of Moral Development.* New York: Harper and Row, 1984.

Kohn, Alfie. "The ABC's of Caring." *Teacher,* 1 (1990), 52–58.

———. "Teaching Children to Care." *Phi Delta Kappan,* 72 (1991), pp. 496–506.

Lickona, Thomas. *Raising Good Children.* New York: Bantam Books, 1983.

Reid, Jo-Anne, Peter Forrestal, and Jonathan Cook. *Small Group Learning in the Classroom.* Scarborough, West Australia: Chalkface Press, 1989.

Schmuck, Richard A. and Patricia A. Schmuck. *Group Processes in the Classroom.* Dubuque, IA: Wm. C. Brown, Company, 1983.

Schniedewind, Nancy. *Cooperative Learning, Cooperative Lives.* Dubuque, IA: Wm. C. Brown, Company, 1983.

Sharan, Shlomo. *Cooperative Learning, Theory, and Research.* New York: Praeger, 1990.

Teacher Resource Books

Baratta-Lorton, Mary. *Mathematics Their Way.* Menlo Park, CA: Addison-Wesley Publishing Company, 1976.

Burns, Marilyn. *About Teaching Mathematics, A K Through 8 Resource.* White Plains, NY: Cuisenaire Company of America, 1992.

———. *A Collection of Math Lessons from Grades 3 Through 6.* White Plains, NY: Cuisenaire Company of America, 1987.

———. *Math by All Means, Multiplication: Grade 3.* White Plains, NY: Cuisenaire Company of America, 1991.

Burns, Marilyn and Cathy McLaughlin. *A Collection of Math Lessons from Grades 6 Through 8.* White Plains, NY: Cuisenaire Company of America, 1990.

Burns, Marilyn, and Bonnie Tank. *A Collection of Math Lessons from Grades 1 Through 3*. White Plains, NY: Cuisenaire Company of America, 1988.

Collis, Mark and Joan Dalton. *Becoming Responsible Learners: Strategies for Positive Classroom Management*. Portsmouth, NH: Heinemann Educational Books, Inc., 1990

Dalton, Joan. *Adventures in Thinking: Creative Thinking and Cooperative Talk in Small Groups*. South Melbourne, Australia: Thomas Nelson Australia, 1990.

EQUALS. *Get It Together: Math Problems for Groups, Grades 4 Through 12*. Berkeley, CA: Lawrence Hall of Science, University of California, 1989.

Freeman, Marji. *Creative Graphing*. New Rochelle, NY: Cuisenaire Company of America, 1986.

Gibbs, Jeanne, and Andre Allen. *Tribes: A Process for Peer Involvement*. Santa Rosa, CA: Center Source Publications, 1987.

Graves, Ted, and Nan Graves. *A Part to Play: Tips, Techniques and Tools for Learning Cooperatively*. Victoria, Australia: Latitude Publications, 1990.

Hosie, Barbara. *Maths About Me*. Melbourne, Australia: Longman Cheshire Pty Limited, 1991.

Kagan, Spencer. *Cooperative Learning*. San Juan Capistrano, CA: Resources for Teachers, Inc., 1992.

Lappan, Glenda, William Fitzgerald, Elizabeth Phillips, Janet Shroyer and Mary Jean Winter. *Middle Grades Mathematics Project*. Menlo Park, CA: Addison-Wesley Publishing Company, 1986. A series of five books for grades 6 through 9.

Meyer, Carol and Tom Sallee. *Make It Simpler: A Practical Guide to Problem Solving*. Menlo Park, CA: Addison-Wesley Publishing Company, 1983.

Morman, Chuck, and Dee Dishon. *Our Classroom: We Can Learn Together*. Portage, MI: The Institute for Personal Power, 1983.

Rhodes, Jacqueline, and Margaret E. McCabe. *The Nurturing Classroom*. Willits, CA: ITA Publications, 1988.

Richardson, Kathy. *Developing Number Concepts Using Unifix Cubes*. Menlo Park, CA: Addison-Wesley Publishing Company, 1984.

Russell, Susan Jo, Rebecca Corwin and Susan Friel. *Used Numbers: Real Data in the Classroom*. Palo Alto, CA: Dale Seymour Publications, 1990. A series of six books for grades K through 6.

Stenmark, Jean, K., Virginia Thompson and Ruth Cossey. *Family Math*. Berkeley, CA: Lawrence Hall of Science, University of California, 1986.

Wilson, Jeni and Peter Egeberg. *Co-operative Challenges and Student Investigations*. South Melbourne, Australia: Thomas Nelson Australia, 1990.